PRAISE FOR *THE THING BENEATH THE THING*

"Some books have the potential to literally save your leadership (and your life). This is one of them. Piercing, scary, genuinely laugh-out-loud funny, and completely disarming, *The Thing Beneath the Thing* will take you places you don't want to go but absolutely need to go."

—Carey Nieuwhof
Bestselling author, podcaster, and speaker

"My brother Steve Carter is a gifted archaeologist of the soul. There's so much that's inside all of us: both beauty and brokenness, pain and hope. Some of it is buried deep. And it takes a trusted, skilled, and seasoned guide to lovingly help us discover not just what's there, but what's possible. Steve is that guide. He doesn't invite you just to look at the dusty, hollow bones of your mess, but to discover the fullness of who God longs for you to be on full display: out of the hole and wholly into the light. This journey of *The Thing Beneath the Thing* will require a willing heart—and Steve Carter has gone first, giving the fullness of his heart to us."

—Ashlee Eiland
Pastor, Mars Hill Bible Church and author of *Human(Kind)*

"Steve wrote the book I wish I had to guide me years ago. If you want to live an authentic life, an actual Jesus-centered life, and a life that is truly healed and whole, this is for you. Filled with hope, humor, and a whole lot of grace, this is a book you'll want to return to again and again and give to everyone you know who wants real freedom."

—Hosanna Wong
International speaker, spoken-word artist, and author of *How (Not) to Save the World*

"Steve Carter is a guide, a sage, a man who has seemingly lived this life before. We all need them, but very few of us have them—people like Steve. As soon as I picked up this book, I couldn't put it down. *The Thing Beneath the Thing* is raw yet relatable, real yet reasonable. Steve provides a playbook on how to handle our emotions, both spoken and unspoken. How to lead with courage and address the areas in our lives that we've been afraid to talk about. He helps us heal. Leaders and followers, both young and old, need this book. Men, women, and children need this book. I need this book. Thank you, Steve, for being courageous enough to go there."

—Sam Acho
Author, speaker, nine-year NFL veteran

"Steve Carter hits the bullseye in this riveting book. Why do we do what we do? Steve expertly unpacks how to identify the source of our behaviors, which, he explains, is ironically the best way to uncover our truest selves! This beautiful truth is shared with wisdom, grace, and humor. I laughed and cried! This book sparked a longing in me for a deep and honest life. These truths will help us all live the life we've been made for."

—Danielle Strickland
Speaker, trainer, global social justice advocate,
and author of *Better Together*

"Steve is the guide that many of us have been searching for and are finally discovering. His words have spoken so much truth into my life over the past few years, and now, with the release of *The Thing Beneath the Thing*, Steve will send those words of healing into the hearts of thousands. I'm certain that healing and freedom will follow every single human who digests them."

—Carlos Whittaker
Speaker, author of *Enter Wild*, and host of *The Human Hope* podcast

"When I think of healthy leadership and leaders who can help me work on that, Steve Carter is one of the first names to come to mind. So for him to write a book on the layers below our decisions, emotions, and directions is a blessing—to all of us. This book is a must-read for anyone, especially a leader, helping them to grasp those things lurking deeply that will allow them to fall or push them to succeed."

—Tyler Reagin
Founder of Life-Giving Company, author, and cofounder of 10TEN Project

THE THING BENEATH THE THING

THE THING BENEATH THE THING

What's Hidden Inside (and What God Helps Us Do About It)

STEVE CARTER

Foreword by Ann Voskamp

W Publishing Group

An Imprint of Thomas Nelson

Library of Congress Control Number: 2021934627

ISBN 978-0-7852-3553-8 (HC)
ISBN 978-0-7852-3560-6 (audiobook)
ISBN 978-0-7852-3559-0 (eBook)

Printed in the United States of America

21 22 23 24 25   LSC   10 9 8 7 6 5 4 3 2 1

To Sarah Lynn,
words can never fully describe who you are and
what you truly mean to me. WATW.

CONTENTS

FOREWORD

BENEATH THE SURFACE OF ALL THINGS IS THE REAL HEART of things—and this will always surface, one way or another.

This you know.

Which may be why you're wisely holding this book, this key, in your hands right now. How can you come to understand what is happening underneath the surface of your only life? Why do we wake with great intentions, visions of thriving relationships and flourishing dreams, and yet someone obliviously says something, or something unexpectedly happens, and we stumble and fall—and why do we do the same thing again tomorrow and, yet again, fall hard?

You must know this: in the deep of the New Zealand forest, a kauri tree fell.

Kauri trees are known to grow to be giants, the tallest of which is known as the "Lord of the Forest," standing at a staggering 168 feet high, with a stretching 115-foot-wide canopy. Who knows exactly why this one particular kauri tree fell hard in the forest? Lightning?

Disease? Cut down in its prime? Whatever the reason, the rains came and fell on the forest floor. The dark nights shrouded the forest in a returning blanket of velveted black, and, night after night, far above this fallen kauri tree and its jagged stump, the stars danced and swirled in choreographic grace. Seasons turned. Sun and moon and solar systems spun.[1]

Who knows how many people walked by that unremarkable stump in the New Zealand forest for years? It looked—dead. A hollowed-out half-cylinder, hardly the size of a chair, the stump looked like a leaf-less, unwelcome eruption in the middle of a hiking trail. A dead and hollowed-out shell of its former, thriving, flourishing self. Perhaps you know in your weary bones that of which we speak?

But it happened on an ordinary day, much like this one, that an ecologist named Sebastian Leuzinger was out for a forest ramble—what the Japanese like to call forest bathing, but what I like to call a daily glory soak, as the whole earth is full of His glory, and what literally cleanses our hearts and minds is a long soak outside under the glory of tree limbs and open sky. Leuzinger spotted the seemingly dead kauri tree stump—only to notice the seemingly impossible.

The stump was dripping sap.

Dead trees don't have sap running through them. Could the cut-down, seemingly very dead stump actually be alive?

Leuzinger leaned over and knocked on the stump. It didn't sound like dead wood.

What in the actual world is going on beneath the world we can see? What actually is going on beneath all the things?

Eventually, after much considered study, the ecologist Leuzinger discovered something rather miraculous: Yes, the stump was definitely alive; yes, the stump had running sap—and yes, the stump still lived because, deep under the earth, far beneath the surface of things, the roots of the stump were wrapped around and connected to, interlaced with, linked to the roots of the forest trees around it.

What the ecologist discovered was that "the tree stump's roots have been grafted together with roots from other trees, something that is known to happen when trees sense they can share resources with the trees around them."[2]

Sense it right now, wherever you unexpectedly find yourself: *you are not alone.*

No matter what things look like, no matter what looks dead, no matter what seems like a stump of all kinds of dreams: you are going to be okay, you are going to thrive, you are going to flourish, you're going to rise from this floor.

Deep underneath that New Zealand forest floor, where no one could see, there was a great grafting weave of roots, a great dance of water flowing, renewing, reviving, restoring. Deep beneath the surface of things, there can be a dance of entwined roots, there can be an intimate connection of giving and sharing resources and supporting.

You are not alone.

While ecologists call this phenomenon a wood-wide web, we can call a similar church-wide phenomenon the Word-wide web: Rooted in the Word, we reach out to each other, live cruciform, live the Word, and create a web that catches all the falling with a love that revives us into a new way of being. The thing beneath our thing can change, because grace can change us, grace can change the fabric of our relationships, grace can change the world, especially ours, especially now.

Beneath the carpet of that kauri forest, roots were grafting mysteriously to other roots, and this stabilized and steadied each tree—and these grafted roots became this hidden dance of givenness where water is shared during hardship. Though you are daily facing your own hardships, though you may feel like the dreams and hopes for your life, your calling, your relationships, have been unexpectedly cut down or that there are ways in which you are a stump of who you dreamed you would always be, the reality is that in this moment you are holding this book. The sap of hope still runs.

The deep, Christ-rooted wisdom of Steve Carter on these pages is like a strong root that will graft around your questions, and the gospel-saturated, strikingly helpful resources he shares with you will revive you. I know—because on more days than I can number, Steve has been exactly this for me. His cruciform faithfulness has supported, his kind grace has steadied, and his strength in Christ and strong, unwavering belief in growth, new possibilities, and fresh mercies has profoundly stabilized me. Whatever forest floor you're walking through, whatever keeps painfully shifting under your feet, Steve Carter is a trusted guide to help you discover what is happening underneath the ground of your relationships, in the fertile dirt of your desires, in the soil of your soul.

The sages know that transformation comes from excavation.

This is why you are here.

Only the excavated life can lay the foundation to build a good life.

Turn these pages and turn over the veneer of things and begin to get down to the thing underneath the thing. Because it's true: Walk through the forest, and each tree may look like it's standing alone—but beneath the earth are roots grafted together into community.

You are not alone.

Forests are made of more than independent trees—forests are made of dependent roots. Trees only stand independent because they're rooted in a shared dependence.

Beneath the surface of things, when our roots are grafted together, we can serve each other living hope in the face of the death of hopes and let the sap of new ways of being begin to run. When there is drought or hardships—the trees that survive are connected to each other in a servant dance of caring fellowship. Which is exactly how you will find Steve's heart, companionship, and wisdom on these deeply life-giving pages.

Underneath the everyday hard, beaten paths of our lives, when our roots are grafted together in Christ, we are rooted no matter what.

And just like all around, overhead, and underneath that fallen kauri tree, with its truncated stump, is what is really happening all around you right now that perhaps you don't see—this Great Cosmic Dance of Love, the Hope and Shalom of the kingdom of God breaking in.

The thing that's deepest underneath everything is always *hope.*

Believe. *And begin.*

—ANN VOSKAMP

MY MOMENT OF MADNESS

A FEW YEARS BACK, WHILE MY WIFE, SARAH, AND I WERE in the process of selling our Grand Rapids house in anticipation of a move to Southern California, we spent an evening sharing a meal with my grandparents. When snow flurries began to fall, Sarah and I put on our jackets and loaded our eight-month-old into our Honda Civic, determined to get safely home before the storm set in. As I drove, a huge chunk of ice hit our windshield, cracking it.

Startled, I swerved. The car slid across the icy street and came to rest on the opposite shoulder. In a state of shock, we tried to figure out what had just happened. Where had that chunk of ice come from?

Then it occurred to me. Someone had thrown it.

I quickly turned the car around, heading back to where the ice had landed. I pulled over, unbuckled, and leapt from the car. "I'm going to find them!" I shouted back to my stunned wife.

Off in the distance, I could make out figures running. "I see you!" I screamed. "I'm calling 911 right now!"

I ran until I came to an embankment. Assuming it was filled with snow, I channeled my inner athlete and attempted to jump over it. I quickly realized that instead of snow it was a puddle of icy water. Could I make it across?

Nope. I landed smack in the middle of it. So now I was soaking wet, freezing, and getting madder by the second. "You can't get away from me!" I yelled, crawling out of the embankment and resuming my chase.

After running across a field, I came to a neighborhood. I stopped in the middle of the street and, because I watched *CSI* religiously, closed my eyes and listened.

Immediately I heard the growl of a garage door three houses down. I ran straight to the front door and rang the doorbell. At this point, I was completely worked up, going over everything I wanted to yell at the person once the door opened. The crack in my windshield. The ice-soaked run. The wife and son left behind on the side of the road. I was so ready to let this guy have it.

But an older gentleman answered the door. "Hello?"

Breathing hard, I quickly asked, "Did some guy just run in here?"

He replied that he'd been home but that his grandson and a friend had just come back in.

I tried to keep my voice calm. "Can I talk to them?"

Moments later, two junior-high boys walked up to the front door, eyes wide, knees shaking, and obviously scared out of their minds. At this point I heard the Spirit of God whisper, *Who is the crazy one here, you or them? Your wife and son are on the side of the road in a snowstorm, and you're standing here with soaking-wet pants about to yell at some kids.*

And then the kicker. *What's really going on, Steve?*

Standing on that welcome mat, eye to eye with those two freaked-out students, I had a moment of clarity. I took a deep breath. "Nice shot," I said simply and then turned back toward the car. With my legs nearing frostbite, I meditated on the question of what was really going on with me.

In truth, I was grieving. Preparing for a big move. Saying goodbye to friends and family. And just hours earlier, I'd found out the buyers for our house had backed out. These things were taking up space in my head and heart, and they were looking for an outlet. What I didn't know at the time was that there were also deep, dark places hidden away in my heart. Experiences I had not fully realized, hurts that had formed deep crevices in my soul. These, along with my inability to trust God with my sadness and disappointment, had led me to give over precious inner territory to a rival force. And now I was acting like a wild man.

The next day I called my mentor and told him about my moment of madness. He laughed. "Welcome to the thing beneath the thing," he said. "Welcome to the endless discovery of what's really going on."

PART ONE

THE SETUP THAT SETS YOU OFF

01

WHY DO I DO THOSE THINGS I DO?

Same as it ever was.

—TALKING HEADS, "ONCE IN A LIFETIME"

I do not understand what I do.

—THE APOSTLE PAUL, ROMANS 7:15

WHEN HEARING ABOUT THE MORAL DOWNFALLS OF celebrities, pro athletes, government officials, pastors, or even neighbors, do you ever find yourself wondering aloud, "What were they thinking?"

It's hard to imagine someone hopping out of bed one morning after hitting snooze a couple of times and saying, "Today's the day! Today I'm going to completely sabotage all the good in my life and wreck my career, forfeit my integrity, and damage the relationships that mean the most to me."

I think we all can agree that doesn't happen. So then, why do those things come to pass again and again, over and over?

Is the answer as simple as what Paul decreed almost two millennia ago? "I do not understand what I do. For what I want to do I do not do, but what I hate I do" (Rom. 7:15).

Is there no understanding for the choices we make? Can it be that life is just a thing that happens to us, and we are unable to control our physical and emotional behaviors?

Really?

Over the last decade, I've become fascinated by this question of why people do regrettable things. Or, better said, why do *I* do what I do?

I've discovered there is always more at play than meets the eye. We can't presume to know what makes us or others tick. The more

I grow in faith and self-awareness, the more I'm beginning to see up close that . . .

We are all mysterious and wild, a collection of sounds and stories inscribed over the years.

We are all made up of hopes, fears, and desires.

We are all products of the messages of love and shame we've received.

We are all full of energy, excitement, and oh so many feels.

It's who I am.

It's who you are.

Sacred and holy.

The weight of feeling not enough and way too much—often in the very same breath.

Every room you walk into, you bring this.

Your whole self.

All of you.

Yet most of the time you and I are unable to locate and identify what is churning within. Like shadows that follow us, our outward attitudes and actions reflect the steps our internal worlds set. We have become functional yet disconnected. Efficient yet unaware. Our bodies carry both truths and lies—every narrative we have ever been subjected to.

Fiction as well as nonfiction.

The body knows.

It holds.

It controls—all of us, until we honor its whole truth.

Where Are You, Really?

We often work to silence and distract ourselves. We escape to those things that we've learned can temporarily soothe us and create distance from the pain or sadness or shame we feel. A dear friend of mine once shared that his first recollection as a child was of falling, scraping his knee, and crying. Jared walked to his mom with both arms raised, looking to be held and comforted. Instead his mom handed him an OREO and told him to stop crying.

Just imagine it. Longing for the embrace of a parent and being handed fifty calories of milk's favorite cookie to make the pain go away. That day began Jared's lifelong battle of turning to food as the magic solution to make everything feel okay inside whenever he encountered painful experiences.

Some of you might be thinking, *Come on, man. There are much worse things that can happen to a kid than being handed a cookie.* But here's the deal: Kids are perceptive. They're just not the best interpreters of reality. Without helpful guides and mentors, they're left trying to make sense of and tangibly apply new information on their own. Sadly, the majority of the time, people grow up returning again and again to these unhelpful patterns of thinking and behaving. Richard Rohr wrote, "Using a scapegoat is our much-preferred method. We deny our pain, sins, and suffering and project them elsewhere. This ancient method still works so well that there is no reason to think it is going to end or change. Until we are enlightened by grace, we don't even see it; it remains safely hidden in the unconscious where it plays itself out."[1]

One OREO became the genesis of an ongoing unhealthy, intimate relationship with food that lasted years. This relationship sabotaged opportunities for connection with actual living humans. Until he was retrained to enjoy a healthy relationship with food, Jared felt powerless in situations of struggle, loss, and trauma. Patterns formed as a child seeking comfort eventually lead to broken relationships, significant isolation, and cycles of deep sin.

But if you had met Jared back then, before he identified what was really going on, you wouldn't have had a clue he was struggling in these ways. By all accounts, he seemed fine. Totally together. You would have had no reason to conclude that his relationship with food was holding him back from true intimacy.

And neither would he. When Jared and I first started meeting to discuss his commitment issues, food wasn't even on the radar. It took months for that realization to factor into our conversations.

Welcome to the thing beneath the thing.

Ten years ago, my wife wanted us to try a full-body detox for a few days. I said sure, not realizing what I was getting myself into. A "few days" turned into twenty-eight days of removing everything that tasted good from our diet. A month of flavorless soup. Smoothies that rivaled composted trash, liquified. I'm not being dramatic. It was bad.

About a week into this experiment, we became increasingly irritable. More tired. More emotional. What was happening?

Apparently the food we'd been putting into our bodies affected more than just our waistbands. And a lifetime of certain foods had made our bodies dependent on them. As we began to expel these toxins, the process became more holistic. All facets were affected—not just the physical, but the mental and emotional too.

Specifically, when I removed soda from my regular diet, I became aware of how much I depended on the sugar and caffeine to give me that extra boost to make it through. Every day around 3:15 p.m., I would drink a can of Dr. Pepper (i.e., the nectar of the gods). Without even realizing it, I'd become reliant on this pick-me-up. My dependency was not on the Holy Spirit to give me strength. Instead, my holy trinity was Father, Son, and Dr. Pepper.

Taking soda away absolutely wrecked me for the first few weeks and sent shock waves throughout my system. My joints ached. My body was fatigued. And every Sarah McLachlan dog commercial had me in tears. This was a strange wake-up call. Until that detox, I had no idea I was using substances to avoid parts of my life. I began to wonder, *What other mediums am I attached to? What, other than the Spirit, am I using to feed, comfort, soothe, numb, and help me escape my actual life?*

So, I took inventory:

Food.
Clothes.
Experiences.
Wine.
Sex.
Influence.
Opportunity.
People.
Achievement.
Money.
Approval.
Comparing.
Goals.
Villainizing.

What would happen if I replaced these things with the goodness of God? Would his peace truly be enough? I wasn't so sure. I really enjoyed Dr. Pepper.

For the first time in a long while I was in touch with my body, my feelings, my sadness. The deeper parts of me.

And I absolutely hated it.

For years, I had functioned from a place of detachment from this deeper self, wanting to silence the voices of contempt, numb the grief

I had stored up, and escape. I'll save that story for another time, but suffice it to say, I was messed up.

So I'd made myself busy.

Or bought something on a credit card with money I didn't have.

I ran to food to soothe and drinks to comfort.

I lost myself in social media.

I villainized those who appeared further along—anything to excite the imagination and lead me away from me.

I hurt those closest to me by constantly overpromising and underdelivering, only to later apologize. I expected my simple "I'm sorry" to make things better, but without committing to change, nothing changed for good.

All the while I was unaware that my behaviors reflected my attempts to cover up agony. That I was afraid to let my true self be truly seen.

I siphoned the good out of an object, experience, or person to feed my needs, then moved on. Buying a new pair of shoes wasn't about delight; it was pure escape. Yet the pain became even louder, like an untamed beast raging out of control. As a result, my desire to numb out only became greater.

I became even busier.

Sought bigger stages.

More success.

More approval.

More food.

More sex.

More fuel for my sin strongholds.

Less awareness of my true need to be seen and loved.

Even less awareness of the grace that was readily available if I would only surrender to it.

Until I derived this revelation by removing Dr. Pepper from my diet. How's that for an aha moment? During this season, I wrote in my journal something I sensed God whispering to me: *How is life working for you?*

How is life working for your pace?

How is life working for your stress?

How is life working for your friendships?

How is life working for your marriage?

How is life working for your heart?

How is life working for your soul?

All I could write in response was, "It's just *not*. I need help."

My friend, how is life working for you?

Unfortunately, many of us are merely existing, relying on toxic tools to keep us insulated from feeling much. Without awareness and intentionality, we'll keep feeding our sin strongholds. Using sugar and caffeine to get through an afternoon slump isn't such a big deal, right? Except that, for some of us, our consumption may be about more than that. It might point to underlying turmoil and some pretty deep wounds. On the surface, you see a guy drinking soda again. Or gaming on his phone again. Or detailing his car again. But underneath, there's a person disconnecting from his truest self.

We all do this, with similar yet different variations. Soothe. Distract. Numb. Escape our negative feelings. These actions take us right back to the very beginning. To the story of God and the time when a man and a woman were running through a garden, looking for a place to hide from him. They'd heard God moving toward them through the lush foliage and ducked behind a tree. But God called out, "Where are you?" (Gen. 3:9).

He wasn't inquiring about their GPS location.

He knew where they were, physically.

He was asking something more profound.

God wanted the man and woman to feel him questioning, *Where are my image-bearers? Where is the fullest expression of who I intended you to be? Where are you, really?*

He didn't want the version of them that was living in fear and shame, hiding from their true selves, their deep-feeling hearts, and their emotional struggles. After all, he'd promised to walk with them through all of that.

He wanted them. The real them. The messy them.

The people he created and cherished.

So where are you, really? Friend, my hope is that in the pages ahead, you'll be emboldened to respond. Because how we live in relation to this simple question will dictate how much we experience the beauty of grace, peace, and wholeness.

You may think you've found the ultimate cocktail that will keep you safe from pain and sadness: striving, curating, performing, numbing. But it does not really exist. At least, not this side of heaven.

Pain is part of living, part of being human. And it's not meant to drive us into hiding behind a flowering fruit tree. Its purpose is to draw us closer to the heart of God.

What Are We So Afraid Of?

Sarah is usually the one who takes the kids to their well-child exams. So as I drove my daughter, Mercy, to the doctor for her four-year checkup, she was already nervous. Maybe her dad wouldn't be up to the challenge. Truth be told, I wasn't so sure myself.

When the time came for her shots, she turned to me, crying. "Don't let them do this to me, Daddy!" That plea shot straight to my gut. What

I wanted to do was push the needle-toting nurse out of the way, grab Mercy in my arms, and be the hero my daughter thinks I am. But I knew the medicine would help her body become stronger and fight sickness in order for her to thrive. So instead, I made her the only promise I could.

"Sis, it's going to hurt for a little while, but it won't hurt forever. You are brave and strong, and here's what I can promise you: I will be right here, and I will not leave you."

Sometimes, we have to go through the painful thing in order to get to the other side. In order to live. In order to thrive. Our instinct to protect ourselves and those we love from pain is good and natural but not always beneficial. What matters is that we know deep down we are strong enough to go through the pain, and we are not alone.

What are you most afraid of?

Whenever we don't face this question head-on, we tend to keep going through those motions of avoidance we set for ourselves early on. As my wife often says, "We do what we want to do." Ultimately, we stay stuck in patterns that aren't best for us because we don't want to do the work to find a better way. Sometimes we try another way only to quit when the going gets too hard, too vulnerable, too messy. And we end up right back in our old, unhealthy habits. We do what we want to do, what we've conditioned ourselves to do, until we get curious, and maybe even a little furious, about why we keep ending up in the same place.

Have you ever been there? Maybe you said something, and the words came out with a surprising amount of edge or cynicism. You wished you could hit the delete button, but it was too late. On the drive home you spent a few minutes reflecting and realized you had been gripped by insecurities. So you'd tried to portray yourself as smarter than the others.

Or maybe you promised yourself you wouldn't have a second drink, but now it's the morning after and your hangover is raging. Or you swore you wouldn't end up going home with that person who wasn't good for you, only to wake up with regret, realizing you did. As you picked up your clothes off the carpet, got dressed, and splashed cool water on your face, did you catch that glimpse in the mirror of your true self staring back?

The way we feel in these moments is a clue to the reality that there is more going on than meets the eye. We're going to take a close look at how underlying triggers may be at play. Most of the time we're unaware we're being triggered. But inside each of us, there are walls being constructed and demolished with every sentence and experience we encounter.

If you don't work to become aware of the thing beneath the thing, your life will stay the same. Your potential, the beauty that is begging to be unleashed within you, will be stunted.

The Other Side of Pain

I remember the exact moment when I knew Sarah was the one. I had been sitting in her college dorm room, surrounded by a sense of grace that made me feel unusually safe. When she asked me a few personal questions, I did something I had never done before. I shared some of my story. I let her see a glimpse of the pain I normally kept deeply buried. I walked back to my apartment feeling the sheer energy of being seen as well as an intense terror of being found out.

I had let down my guard, and I never did that. For a moment, I'd stopped exhibiting an image and just let myself be. In a matter of about ninety minutes, Sarah had discovered the passcode and penetrated the walls of security I'd spent years constructing. What was I in for now?

Turned out, I was in for a lifetime of truth telling, love, and adventure. And all of it would be, at times, scary as hell.

Inside you, at every moment, it's all there. The joy and the pain. The delight and the fear. The desire to be seen and the impulse to hide.

I believe God wired us and empowers us to be beings of awareness. He gifted each of us with the ability to discern, to see beyond, to dream for more, to create safety nets for ourselves and one another.

A few years back, after an early morning walk, I was replaying a conversation I'd had with my wife. I say conversation, but really it took a turn from dialogue to argument. And in that moment I chose something other than God's best. As I was processing through this with God, I discovered something that forever changed the way I understand myself. This, my friend, is *THING*.

Triggers: the setup that sets us off

Hideouts: the metaphoric places we go to escape the pain of our story

Insecurities: the false stories we create about ourselves

Narratives: the false stories we create about others

Grace: the ongoing process and spiritual power that makes us whole, holy, and spiritually healthy

Here is the reality: as a human on this planet interacting daily with other humans on this planet, I will experience being triggered multiple times a day. So will you. And each time we will be presented with a choice.

After walking and reflecting a bit, I found a bench and sat down to list my known triggers. This was sort of like taking inventory of those moments in my days that trip me up, change my attitude, or alter my mood. A plethora of things does this. But triggers don't stop there. No, we go to other "places" to try to deal with our discomfort, and they're often unhealthy. In the pages ahead, we'll talk about these hideouts.

For now, it's enough to begin thinking about our triggers.

For example, I'm triggered when I fail at something. When I become embarrassed and my competitive ego is hurt.

I'm triggered when I'm caught by surprise. When I feel like I've lost control of my situation and I'm no longer sure how to meet everyone's expectations.

I'm triggered by loneliness.

I'm triggered by glimpses of pride in another person, when I lose sight of the imago Dei, the image of God, in them.

I'm triggered by others' disapproval of or anger at me.

Friends, when we get triggered—and we will—we are going to go somewhere with our emotional discomfort. I wonder: Where do you go? What are the hideouts, insecurities, and false narratives you most often run to? And to what level have you allowed the healing power of God's generous grace into your story?

To answer these questions, we'll need to muster up a profound level of curiosity to dig even deeper. Why, we have to wonder, do certain things uniquely trigger us in the first place? If triggers are behind our unhealthy responses, what is the even more foundational thing behind our triggers?

The thing beneath the thing.

Spiritual poets Father Thomas Keating and Mary Mrozowski taught me to respond to my growing curiosity by saying, "Welcome, welcome, welcome. I welcome everything that comes to me in this moment because I know it is for my healing."[2] Indeed, learning to tune in to our internal goings-on is a God-given gift. In effect we have our very own internal thermometers that read the feelings, emotions, and safety of a room. Just like you have a set temperature for your house, your body has been trained to maintain a set internal temperature. This is what psychologists refer to as your homeostasis. Your everyday normal. It's where you feel most comfortable to breathe, move, and live.

Have you ever met someone who feels more at ease in stress?

Or someone who shuts down the moment there is a hint of conflict?

Or someone who seems to consistently choose to stay in dysfunction?

Or someone who dances around the chaos of another?

Or someone who dates a great partner but finds a way to wreck the relationship?

Or someone who just goes and goes and goes and never really sits still?

Or someone who can't seem to handle money or a schedule or hold down a job?

Our internal temperatures are like a default setting that we know how to navigate with our eyes closed. They're often not the best for our souls or a thriving relationship with Christ, but they are the setting where we feel most familiar.

This familiar position keeps us feeling in control, allowing us to manage our pain and safeguard from more disappointments. It's a survival tactic, and for times of struggle, it can serve to keep us alive. But as we grow, we change. What worked to keep us safe during a crisis won't work for us as we step into a life of wholeness. If we stay in what's comfortable, we are unable to receive the full love, grace, and peace God has for us on the other side of pain.

The problem is that most of us tend to re-create that familiar position in every environment we enter into. We know how to navigate it, so we project it onto our current situation.

I don't know how to exist well in situations where I'm not expected to overachieve. I don't know how to rest well. I tend to take a good thing and strive to make it the best thing ever. And usually when I do this, I end up missing out on the simple joy of the moment. But I know how to operate within a framework of stress and striving. I can do it with my eyes closed. And if I'm not careful, I will reconstruct this kind of framework over and over for the rest of my life.

You, too, have a familiar default position. Do you know what it is? Are you willing to uncover it?

Until you honor this truth, your life will be held in check. How can you embrace the unknown if you are always trying to re-create the known? The kindness of God is the invitation to get after the thing beneath the thing so you can discover an entirely new frontier of life, blessing, and God's nearness.

How to Benefit from This Book

Think of this book as simply a walk I've invited you to take with me for a short while. Together we will look at the parts of our stories where perhaps emotional potholes have been formed by pain, trauma, or choices we've made. We'll examine where God, in his kindness, is trying to fill them up with his grace and love.

I can't promise you it will be easy or simple. You're going to experience profound moments of vulnerability, and there may be times you'll want to stop altogether. The promise I'm making you is that I will be beside you in spirit, my words and story serving as a map, a way through the challenges we're bound to encounter as we dig deeper. This journey will invite you to grab hold of courage, to take an honest look at what you've long been harboring inside. The payoff is, of course, that you will unlock parts of your soul and calling that have long been buried. Stifled dreams will find new breath. Your soul will be unfettered.

And you will be free.

You'll learn to make a regular habit of asking yourself key questions that will unlock those most vulnerable places, the ones we all work so hard to keep buried. If possible, work through this book with a friend or a group. Grab a journal and jot down insights and questions as they come up for you. Make time to sit with your stirred-up feelings and invite trusted community to journey with you.

Are you ready? Let's dig deep and get curious and invite healing and learn new ways to operate.

I believe you're going to grow in ways you may never have imagined for yourself as you begin to truly experience the fullness of life—the joy and freedom Jesus promised.

Let's walk.

DIG A LITTLE DEEPER

1. As you were reading, did any triggers come to mind? Jot those down.
2. What feelings or concerns are stirred up as you prepare to begin this journey?
3. Take a few moments to reflect on the first couple of lines of "The Welcome Prayer," and invite God to walk with you as you begin to dive deep into your story. "Welcome, welcome, welcome. I welcome everything that comes to me in this moment because I know it is for my healing."

02

—

POTHOLES, TRIGGERS, AND RESPONSES

All my lies are always wishes.
—WILCO, "ASHES OF AMERICAN FLAGS"

Be holy in all you do.
—THE APOSTLE PETER, 1 PETER 1:15

YEARS AGO, I HAD SOME REALLY DIFFICULT INTERACTIONS with a coworker. This person was a worrier by nature and a pessimist, a combination that made collaborating incredibly hard for me. I felt like he shot down every idea I shared, and whenever I'd throw out an alternative, he would slam it faster than I could get the words out.

One day I came home from a particularly frustrating meeting with him and unloaded all the gory details on my wife. She sat there and listened to every word, sighed, and then had the audacity to smile. Smile! Now I was getting upset with her too. "Why are you smiling?" I asked, barely masking my dissatisfaction.

She spoke slowly, cautiously. "I just think, babe, that God is so incredibly kind to you." I'd expected her to say a lot of things, but definitely not this. How was placing me in a relationship with this negative person God's way of being kind?

"Listen," Sarah continued, "this guy seems to just bring out the worst in you. I wonder why that is. Maybe something about him is stirring up an old wound for you. What may be buried that God is inviting you to resurrect so you can be wholly healed from it? What do you think?"

I thought many things at that moment. Her words enwrapped me like a thousand-pound weight. They felt heavy because they felt true. This was the God I knew, relentless in his pursuit of our wholeness.

Where we have experienced pain, he desires to heal. Where we have been broken, he wants to mend.

That was the day I began reframing my more challenging interactions with others by expanding them to include curiosity. Curiosity about the possibility that my knee-jerk reactions were actually an inner signaling toward some hidden pain nerve being tapped. Curiosity about what God may be inviting me to bring to light, to make room for him to heal. Indeed, the Lord will use the people and circumstances in our lives to continuously invite us to be open and available to him. Why? So we may grow and heal and become new.

One of the greatest honors of my life has been to sit with people as they've shared their joys and struggles, challenges and regrets, fears and questions. Over time, certain striking similarities have emerged from these conversations. No one ever has said they intended to max out their credit cards, engage in extramarital affairs, or drink so much that they lose control. Of course we don't consciously set out to destroy our lives! These behaviors and outcomes are collateral damage from choices that happened much, much earlier in our stories.

As I counseled and pastored people through their seasons of pain and brokenness, I became super curious about what was behind those initial decisions. And I wondered about this not only in regard to others but also for me personally.

In Romans 2:4 Paul expressed that God's kindness toward you and me is purposed to lead us away from sin, away from feeling we're in any position to judge others. His patience with our blind spots softens our hearts for transformation. Isn't God so kind when he reveals an area in your life that has gone unnoticed to you but not by him? Isn't God so kind in the way he invites you to trust him with that pain and wound?

Sidenote: I want to take a moment to ensure that this isn't an endorsement of abusive behavior. I am not encouraging you to endure an unloving or unsafe relationship, and I am not telling you that you have to forgive someone who is unrepentant or dangerous. If you find yourself in that toxic dynamic, please reach out to someone safe and ask for help. In this context, I'm referring to the people who are merely stepping on our unseen internal land mines, and our reactions are the result of years of untended wounds.

Potholes

You know it's springtime in Illinois when the orange construction barrels are in full bloom. From the earliest moments of sunlight, dedicated construction crews are busy at work. These crews are lifesavers because one of the hardest things to manage in the city is navigating around all the potholes. They're everywhere!

It may sound crazy, but the city of Chicago has a hotline designated exclusively to reporting potholes. And I've even heard rumors that if you and your car have suffered the joy of discovering one, and if the reported pothole isn't fixed in due time, the city will reimburse you for your repairs.

Once during the time we lived there, I hit a pothole while driving downtown. By the sheer *whomping* sound of my front wheel striking the massive crater, I knew I had an instant flat tire. After pulling my car to the nearest shoulder, a quick inspection confirmed my fears.

So, of course, I called the hotline number as fast as I could, hoping for a clerical error that would pay for my tire repair. (No luck there, as things turned out.) While the employee took down my information, we chatted for a few minutes. I asked if she knew the average number of potholes filled by the city each year.

"As a matter of fact," she responded, "the *Chicago Tribune* just did a story on the number repaired in just the first two months of 2018. Do you want to take a guess?"

Since I was waiting for the tow truck driver anyway, I thought I would play along. I hazarded a guess. "Twenty-five thousand?"

"Close, but it's a little more."

"Forty thousand potholes?"

"Getting warmer."

"Fifty thousand!"

"Final answer?" she asked.

"Yes, final answer." *For the love of all that's holy.*

She proceeded to inform me that Chicago had repaired 108,000 potholes in those first few months of the year.[1] Apparently, the city maintains an online "pothole tracker," which gets updated in real time as repairs are made.[2]

Hold on a second, I thought. *The third-largest city in the country has a pothole tracker? What does that even mean? They literally have someone who dedicates their workday to updating pothole locations throughout the city?* I couldn't help but imagine how this might play out for a kindergartener on Take Your Parent to School Day.

First, little Bobby introduces his father. "This is my dad. He plays defense for the Chicago Bears." All the kids clap and start chanting, "Bear down!"

Then little Johnny stands up. "This is my dad. He runs the city of Chicago's pothole tracker!" Pure, unadulterated pandemonium might follow. I imagined kindergarteners absolutely losing their minds, begging for the pothole tracker's autograph. Or then again, maybe not.

Clearly, I'm a weird guy because this little incident inspired a day of research for me. And here's how what I learned about potholes can help each of us think about the thing beneath the thing.

First, a construction crew performs an inspection to determine what caused the hole. The majority of potholes occur when water seeps into the pavement, freezes, and expands. Since asphalt doesn't have elasticity to handle the stretching, a pothole is born. These types of holes are pretty easy to fix. The construction crew simply fills in the gap, updates the pothole tracker, and moves on to the next hole.

But every once in a while, they come to a pothole that wasn't caused by inclement weather. Maybe the culprit was a broken sewage pipe or some other water leak or underground erosion. In these cases, the situation is more serious. The construction crew can't just make a quick patch and move on. First, they must address the problem that caused it. If they try to patch this type of pothole without first solving the thing beneath it causing the damage, the cavity will erode. Eventually, it will grow to become what we know as a sinkhole.[3]

This actually happened a few years ago in Chicago. An entire city block was swallowed up. Multiple cars descended into the earth. Someone was hospitalized. And hundreds of thousands of dollars in damage was sustained.

We all have potholes in our life stories, markings of long-ago emotional pain caused by the hurtful words and behaviors of others. Or perhaps the etchings of shame from decades-old sin. By nature, these potholes are below the surface, so they often go unnoticed. But their existence means that problems are likely to arise. And when our personal potholes are left unaddressed, the potential for unforeseen damage is real.

In and of themselves, Chicago's potholes are inanimate and have no power to do harm—until some oblivious driver crosses their path. In the same way, our personal potholes are just places of scarring along our journey. Until they become triggered.

Triggers

I call internal sensitivities to incidents from our past *triggers* because they usually strike a nerve. And this ignites an action, typically a defensive one.

If our potholes are a collection of key moments we've carried under a shroud of shame and secrecy for a long, long time, triggers are our emotions surrounding those events. When we complain someone is "pushing our buttons," we mean that our potholes have become triggered.

Whenever someone drives near a pothole in our story that hasn't been put right, all those emotional echoes from the past begin to wonder, *Where will we go?*

Where *does* shame go? All that weight and pressure has to go somewhere, doesn't it? When we repress it deep down inside, it takes a toll on us. On our bodies, our spirits, our ability to trust and hope and try new things.

When a person or circumstance brushes up against that scar, you may experience—quite subconsciously, even—emotions associated with an issue you assumed was long under control. Listen, friend: never underestimate the power of an old wound, a painfully traumatic moment from your past that you thought you'd filled in, to send you into a tailspin.

Punchlines and Punching Bags

When I was a kid, few things compared to the feeling of victory I got from making adults laugh. Especially my dad. He was a big guy, hard to impress, and on the rare occasion I could get him really going, I was on top of the world.

Often I would lie in bed, rehearsing a joke over and over until my timing was spot-on. When I was home alone, I would watch and rewatch videos of stand-up comedians or read joke books I borrowed from the library. I had to discover the secrets of comic success. And I had to be sure Dad would laugh.

Here's what I know about telling a great joke. First, you need the audience to buy into it. This requires "taking them on a journey." You want them all in, following closely as you deliver each line. This is a bit like a magician's sleight of hand technique. Everyone is so busy watching the top hat that they don't have a moment to notice the cage out of which you just pulled a rabbit. With a good joke, you don't want anyone seeing where the punchline is coming from.

You get audience buy-in, take them right up to the edge, and then— *bam!*—you change directions. You give the setup, and then you deliver the unexpected.

Setups happen in life, too, but not always with a laugh at the other end. More often than not we can feel we've been set up only to be launched into an unexpectedly difficult situation. In this way, I'd like us to think of triggers as the setup that sets us off.

It's human nature. The setup sets us off to go somewhere.

To escape.

To numb.

To scapegoat.

To rage.

To cry.

To heal.

To soothe.

To distract.

But how does it happen? I see a formula come into play that offers us a choice.

The Formula

While Urban Meyer was head coach of the Ohio State Buckeyes football team, he took a formula coined by Jack Canfield and plastered these words all over the team facilities:

Events + Response = Outcome.

Or simply stated: E + R = O.

The message is this: You and I do not control the *events* of life. Things will happen. You will experience a bad day, a hard phone call, another stock market crash. Or perhaps you will get into a crash. Get a ticket. Miss a deadline or your quarterly projection. You often have zero control over these and countless other things. The only thing you can control is your *response*.

Whatever the event might be, your response to it—the choice you make—determines the *outcome*. Bury your head in the sand, and the problem will still be there. Blame someone else, and you'll have to reconcile your relationship with the person you blamed. In sports, you'll see this happen again and again during a game. A player cheap-shots another player, who reacts. The referee sees the reaction and throws a penalty flag.

This is why coaches preach Canfield's phrase. They need their players to rise above other players' cheap shots and taunts. They want their players to learn that when they are set off, the consequences affect them as well as their team and fans.

The same is true with life. Events happen. We will all get triggered daily, even multiple times a day. And often by the same person or specific kind of situation.

Over and over. Rinse and repeat.

The enemy is looking to set us off.

If we aren't in touch with our triggers, our lives may become an unexpected punchline to others. And those around us may become punching bags.

All because we lacked the courage to get curious.

Let's look at how this plays out in a familiar story from the Old Testament. Chapter 3 of Esther ends on this sentence: "The king and Haman sat down to drink, but the city of Susa was bewildered" (v. 15). The king referred to in this story was a megalomaniac named Xerxes I. Xerxes was as insecure as they come yet extremely powerful. After sending his people into a state of terror and confusion, he sat down for a cocktail with his new right-hand man.

Why was the city of Susa bewildered? The previous two verses detail that dispatches had been sent "by couriers to all the king's provinces with the order to destroy, kill and annihilate all the Jews—young and old, women and children—on a single day, the thirteenth day of the twelfth month, the month of Adar, and to plunder their goods. A copy of the text of the edict was to be issued as law in every province and made known to the people of every nationality so they would be ready for that day" (vv. 13–14).

The locals were reeling at news of a decree: mass genocide. Throughout the Persian Empire, from Ethiopia to India and up to modern-day Pakistan, the Jewish people were to be wiped out.

Over the course of history, many people groups have lived, and too often died, under threat of genocide. In 2002, I was in Rwanda and saw up close the trauma caused when one tribe tries to eliminate another. According to the United Nations, in just one hundred days, approximately eight hundred thousand Rwandans were killed.[4]

It happened in the fifth century BCE, in the twentieth century CE, and throughout human history.

But how had this genocide described in the Bible come to be? What was the thing beneath this awful thing?

Let's back up further in the story. "Then Haman said to King Xerxes, 'There is a certain people dispersed among the peoples in all the provinces of your kingdom who keep themselves separate. Their customs are different from those of all other people, and they do not obey the king's laws; it is not in the king's best interest to tolerate them'" (v. 8).

Tolerate was an interesting choice of words for Haman to use in his statement to King Xerxes. Xerxes' grandfather was a king named Cyrus the Great, a very tolerant king known for creating the first bill of human rights. Whenever he took over various cities and countries, he wouldn't harm the people—he would actually empower them, freeing them to work with him to build the Persian Empire. Yet Haman was insisting Xerxes forget all about his grandfather's legacy, saying:

These people are separate from you.

These people are different from you.

These people don't obey you.

These people don't respect you.

Do not *tolerate* them.

Next, the king's right-hand guy uttered these words: "If it pleases the king, let a decree be issued to destroy them, and I will give ten thousand talents of silver to the king's administrators for the royal treasury" (v. 9).

Haman had not only fabricated this whole story but was also willing to bankroll the genocide. While there is no confirmed count of Jews living in exile throughout the Persian Empire, my conservative estimate based on research I've done is at least one hundred and twenty thousand, which would mean that one talent was worth twelve Jewish lives.

What would compel a person to make such a decree and fabricate such a story?

What would make a man want to bankroll mass murder?

To answer those questions, let's start with the triggers. What set Haman off? Back in verse 2 we read, "All the royal officials at the king's gate knelt down and paid honor to Haman, for the king had commanded this concerning him. *But Mordecai would not kneel down or pay him honor*" (emphasis added).

To pay honor here means to lie prostrate on the ground. Because Haman was the king's top guy, every single place he went, every person in the empire was commanded to fall to the ground out of reverence and respect. Can you even imagine?

Except Mordecai. Mordecai didn't kneel. Mordecai remained standing.

And this did something within Haman. "When Haman saw that Mordecai would not kneel down or pay him honor, he was enraged. Yet having learned who Mordecai's people were, he scorned the idea of killing only Mordecai. Instead Haman looked for a way to destroy all Mordecai's people, the Jews" (vv. 5–6).

Haman brainstormed and financed genocide because a dude wouldn't kneel before him. We don't know all that contributed to his pothole—the lies and wounds that led to Haman's fear and insecurity, all buried under a flimsy layer of pride. But we know Mordecai stepped on it.

Do you see how a pothole can quickly become a sinkhole?

Do you see how a trigger can set someone off?

Do you see the damaging ways E + R = O can play out?

One event, a man unwilling to lie prostrate, triggered a response that nearly led to a deadly outcome.

When you and I get triggered, all that energy from past hurts has to be channeled and transferred somewhere. Friends, we may not be in danger of plotting murder, but if we don't deal properly with our potholes, destructive emotions will take up residency somewhere. And we'll put ourselves and others at risk.

Yet I'm here to say it's more than possible to control our responses when we've been set up to be set off. Doing so is going to require intentionality, a willingness to slow down long enough to get curious about why we are feeling uneasy, and a lot of courage, humility, and patience. And it's going to require God's grace.

The Choice

Do you ever wake up in the morning after overdrinking, overeating, oversharing, or overspending and wonder, *What was I thinking? Why did I do that thing that hurts rather than helps?*

It's the ultimate question, really. The fact is, if we don't take the time to discover honest answers, we risk hurting our relationships not only with ourselves but also with others. What's more, we compromise our credibility as Christ followers with the rest of the world. As a result, our witness as children of God and our lives as examples of the redemptive power of Jesus can suffer. The stakes, my friends, actually could not be any higher.

One of the greatest lies we're sometimes told is that our choices affect only us. We convince ourselves no one else needs to know. *This will be my secret. I can manage this. I can keep it quiet.* But sin always leaves collateral damage. And when your wounds extend beyond just your own story, when your personal potholes turn into sinkholes and shake the lives of those around you, ripples of unnecessary hurt, relational pain, and brokenness follow.

You see, God designed us to live in community. Our entire natural world is spun together in such a way that everything we do, every choice we make, affects those around us. For better and for worse, we belong to one another.

Here's the truth: you may make choices each and every day that bewilder those around you. As you go to bed at night, there may be people wondering why you responded as you did—why you said that thing or acted that way. And I'm willing to bet there are people who perplex you with their choices too.

But if you're like me, you struggle to be holy in every given moment. When I'm triggered by something or someone, I often withdraw and hide out. I usually start assuming I know more than the other person about their motives and make up a storyline that fuels my indignation. The danger to me and to others is real because my response is never just about me. This pattern only grows until it inevitably leaks out to those around me.

Bitterness, anger, insecurity, envy, fear, and resentment (and the motivations behind these emotions) will always manifest in uncontainable, unmanageable ways. Over time, the question becomes not *if* but *when* my responses will hurt my relationships with my partner, my kids, my coworkers, my church community, and so on.

So why do we choose the unholy over the holy?

Even the apostle Paul, a gifted teacher, or *rabbi*, with his advanced knowledge of Torah and Spirit-infused insight into the mind of Christ, admitted to struggling with this conundrum. He said, "I do not understand. . . . For what I want to do I do not do, but what I hate I do" (Rom. 7:15).

Maybe you can relate.

On the bright side, our negative emotions and the resulting responses are divine clues that serve as time-sensitive invitations to turn to God for healing before a pothole becomes a sinful sinkhole. One of Jesus' disciples wrote, "Do not conform to the evil desires you had when you lived in ignorance. But just as he who called you is holy, so be holy in all you do; for it is written: 'Be holy, because I am holy'" (1 Peter 1:14–16). The clarion call from this passage is that we are meant to be set apart, to live a life that is consecrated, on mission, and for a purpose. When we choose holiness, we are living from a spiritually whole and healthy place.

I imagine most of us hear this as good news. We want so desperately for God to redeem every part of our stories, to make the pain disappear, and to help us live more righteous and beautiful lives. Of course we do. But we're also terrified. Because to experience the freedom we desire, we must be willing to get after the thing beneath the thing. Which brings us back to why you and I have embarked on this journey together at this moment in time.

In his kindness, the God of the universe gently offers to attend to our microwounds before things have a chance to go sideways. Paul even already prayed for us! In Philippians 1:4–6 he said, "In all my prayers for all of you, I always pray with joy . . . being confident of this, that he who began a good work in you will carry it on to completion until the day of Christ Jesus."

Buckle up, friends, and let's dig in. Because the only way to reach our goal of authentic healing is to go through and not around that thing we're afraid of. We can trust God. I'm confident of this.

DIG A LITTLE DEEPER

1. What are some of your personal triggers?
2. Can you name the pothole (painful story) that is at the root of what triggers you?
3. If all we control is our response (remember E + R = O), what has been your typical response in health and unhealth when you get triggered?
4. What pothole is God, in his kindness, relentlessly going after right now in your life?

PART TWO

COURAGEOUS CURIOSITY

03
——

WHERE WE GO TO HIDE

Close your eyes and count to ten.
—TOM WAITS, "GEORGIA LEE"

Where are you?
—GOD, GENESIS 3:9

WHEN I WAS A KID, I LOVED PLAYING HIDE-AND-SEEK. I loved the thrill of hiding. Loved that victorious feeling of holding out until my friends gave up and never found me. I would wear that badge of honor for weeks. Ironically, I always returned to the same few spots, which probably said more about their seeking skills than my hiding.

I still find myself scoping out the best hiding spots whenever I walk into a room. My daughter, Mercy, shares a similar love for the game, but she's much smarter than me. When Mercy was four, she created a rule for us: If the seeker can't find the other person, they can shout, "Can I get a tweet-tweet?" The person hiding then makes a *tweet-tweet* sound like a little bird, giving the seeker a clue.

Regardless of who wins, wouldn't we all much rather be the one hiding than the one whose job it is to seek out the holed-up person?

Which raises some interesting questions, doesn't it?

Even at an early age, we instinctively know there's value in being able to hide, escape, and avoid. Sure, we make a game of it, but we also make a lifestyle of it.

A Counterfeit Solution

Throughout history, this lifestyle of avoidance has led to a posture of false appeasement. In the ancient Near East during the time of the exodus, most nations and people groups went to great lengths to keep their gods happy. For example, if their crops needed rain, they might host a festival dedicated to persuading the gods to open up the skies. These gatherings involved chaotic music, wild dancing, and loud chants, accompanied by drum circles (1 Kings 18:20–40). The people would likely engage in excessive sexual acts, cut themselves or one another, and sacrifice animals or even humans. Remember, all of this was just to bring on the rain.

Let's explore why rain was so important. Rain symbolized blessing. Agricultural blessing meant financial blessing, which demonstrated to these nations that their gods were pleased with them. When the rains didn't come, the people would raise the stakes. Beat the drums harder. Chant louder. Dance with more urgency.

Meanwhile the Hebrew people, having just dramatically escaped persecution through miraculous intervention, were wandering in the wilderness, heading toward a land promised to them. But when Yahweh summoned their leader, Moses, to meet with him on top of Mount Sinai, Moses had to leave the people in the hands of his brother, Aaron. As the days and weeks went by, the people began to worry. Where was Moses?

They were no good at waiting, and panic took over. They began telling themselves stories about what could have happened to Moses, which only created more anxiety, until they somehow forgot altogether the miracles that had gotten them this far. And, of course, they had heard all about the pagan festivals their neighbors held. In fact, it's safe to say they'd sometimes heard drumbeats, cheers, and screams nearby. In their anxious state, and with this other idea about how to provoke a god's attention tickling their minds, some began to wonder if they should try it for themselves.

I don't knock them at all, by the way. It's only natural to react with fear when we're at the end of our rope. When our natural tendencies toward worry, doubt, and panic take over, we can find it hard to think with the wisdom a moment demands.

"Come," the people said, gathering around Aaron, "make us gods who will go before us. As for this fellow Moses who brought us up out of Egypt, we don't know what has happened to him" (Ex. 32:1). As the crowd gathered around him, Aaron must have been heavy with despair. He must have wondered where his brother was, just like the others. He must have felt anxious as he imagined the likelihood that he would soon be asked to take Moses' place.

I wonder if, as the mob closed in, he simply reached for the easiest solution to keep the people happy. Perhaps he noticed the sun glinting off golden bangles and earrings all around him and decided to give the people what they wanted, a melted-down minigod to calm their fears. Aaron directed the people to bring all their gold to him, and they quickly obliged. Exodus 32:4 says, "He took what they handed him and made it into an idol cast in the shape of a calf, fashioning it with a tool. Then they said, 'These are your gods, Israel, who brought you up out of Egypt.'" And Aaron declared the next day an epic festival for the gods. The following day, God's chosen people arose ready to kick off the festivities by sacrificing burnt offerings and presenting fellowship offerings. Next they "sat down to eat and drink and got up to indulge in revelry" (Ex. 32:6).

They'd managed to go from sheer panic to revelry. How?

Their shining calf became a thing on which to cast all their distress. A golden opportunity to escape. But in truth it represented a molten concoction of raging anxiety and lack of dependence on God. As Tim Keller would say, it was a counterfeit god. "Idols give us a sense of being in control, and we can locate them by looking at our nightmares. What do we fear the most? What, if we lost it, would make life not worth living? We make 'sacrifices' to appease and please our gods, who we believe will protect us."[1]

We all have these counterfeits. Idols of our own making—interior places we go to hide and vices to soothe us from the harder parts of reality. We're looking for a golden calf to carry it all for us so we don't have to. All of our stresses and struggles, our worries and fears, our shame and our pain. Every unmet expectation, trauma and sin, frustration and failure. Our bitterness. Our despair. Even our existential questions about our worth and our future.

Short-Term Solutions

I'll never forget the first time one of my kids lied to me. I knew they were lying but waited to see if they would do the right thing and tell me the truth. Nope. I was floored as I watched them craft a bold-faced fabrication, a (very) unbelievable story, to cover their tracks. I let it happen, then looked them in the eyes and said, "I am so thankful you would never lie to me. I know you understand the irreplaceable value of trust. And I'm so grateful you would never break that trust with me." Yep, you got it. Dad guilt to the max. But it worked!

Within an hour, my child came downstairs to confess, with big tears and genuine sorrow not only for the original lie but also for the new layers of wrongdoing caused by the deceit. I imagine God operates like this with us. Not the dad-guilt part, of course, but the trust part. He doesn't force truth or manage us as robots. Instead, he lets his children experience the struggle that comes with broken trust, the power of confession, and the heavenly beauty of being forgiven.

And we need to experience this over and over because we humans become increasingly better at hiding as we grow up. As we get older, the risks associated with hiding also grow—in cost and in complexity. We expend a lot of energy trying to manage our secrets and facades. Living under false pretenses, misrepresenting ourselves to our own selves and to others shuts people out. Now we're guarding potholes, and they're becoming bigger, deeper, and more hazardous.

Of course, wherever there is tenderness and internal struggle, there is a predator ready to take advantage. Ready to persuade us we can shortcut the healing process. But instead of being set free, we become caught in an even deeper spiral of shame.

Need an example?

Let's look at the consumer credit industry. What does Chase Bank call its credit card? The Freedom card. *Chase freedom*—get it? Why should you have to wait to get what you want? Don't let anything keep you from your pursuit of happiness! You don't know what the future holds, so you might as well take matters into your own hands. Simply fill the holes in your heart with, well, whatever you want! Never mind the average interest rate of 14.65 percent.[2] Such a small price to pay for the illusion of control, right?

In a brilliant marketing strategy, Chase found a way to sell financial slavery under a banner of freedom.

Credit card companies count on our lack of self-control and our fear. The top ten credit card companies in the United States spent over a combined billion dollars in advertising in 2019.[3] What they're selling is glittery and hard to walk away from because it's designed to remove the agony of waiting. And just like the Hebrew people, who reduced God to a hunk of gold to soothe their anxiety, we find ourselves clicking "add to cart" knowing full well we're paying for wanted items with money we don't actually have. The masterful trick of it is that, for a little while anyway, "retail therapy" really does feel like freedom and escape. But it causes pain in the long run.

What our Freedom card purchased was simply a short-term hiding place. The stuff we collect and surround ourselves with is not innately evil. But just like that hunk of gold formed into the likeness of a cow, our motivation for having something reveals the flaw. When we ask it to provide what it can't deliver—the antidote to our internal discomfort—we spoil the good.

And we're still left with that ominous pothole.

The Surefire Way to Ruin a Good Thing

We all want good things. But it's fairly easy to take a good thing, such as work or money, technology or art, fashion or food, and siphon all the innate goodness out of it, like an addict looking for another hit. Some addictions are more socially acceptable than others, like when I devour an entire carton of ice cream in one evening or binge-watch an entire season of Netflix's latest show or spend hours researching every NFL player for my fantasy football draft.

Consider for a moment how you interact with any of these seemingly innocuous things within a typical month of your life:

- television
- your job
- social media
- travel
- online shopping
- your children
- studying
- serving
- friendships
- food
- sex

Now ask yourself this: *Did I use _____ to escape discomfort or make me feel better about my circumstances?* Even in the last month, most of us would have to admit we have used these kinds of things to soothe us or provide relief from unpleasant experiences. We may even have joked about doing so. Often, though, we aren't even aware we are doing this. Our motives can be subtle, and we typically develop habits over time. Remember, none of the things listed are inherently bad. As C. S. Lewis wrote, "Badness is only spoiled goodness."[4] These choices we make just run the risk of being co-opted for something unhealthy.

Why unhealthy? Whenever Christ invites us to lean in and instead we do all we can to leap out, we forfeit intimacy with him. We are settling for the fast and fake instead of waiting in trust for the real thing. It is much, much harder to slow down, admit a mistake, confess a sin, or let ourselves be seen as less than perfect. Sadly, many of us have received the message that to be loved we must keep parts of ourselves hidden, so we work to conceal those parts. As much as we desire the transforming power of Jesus to do a new work in us, this takes time, intentionality, and honesty.

Yet Jesus waits with tenderness and patience.

Meanwhile, our society celebrates quick success and instant gratification.

If we keep our secrets well enough—if we perfect our facade—we advance, we are celebrated, and our influence grows. But all the while, we may be ducking the reality of our circumstances. The potholes slowly grow and become dangerously close to turning into sinkholes. Don't forget, friends, that we are really good at hiding.

Once triggered, we're launched into one of three major defenses. We tend to (a) hide and pretend, (b) become insecure, or (c) make up narratives to help us feel better. Or some combination of all three.

None of these is as obvious as it sounds, and each is loaded with unforeseen tension, challenge, and sin. When we get triggered, a raw, internal, deeply emotional horsepower is unleashed, a rush of energy that needs to go somewhere fast.

Anthropologists have long studied the human tendency to react to a threat via one of three modes: fight, flight, or freeze. When we don't have the tools to accomplish a better response, when we lack the map to show us how to best move forward in health, we run the risk of having our emotions make the calls.

Desire. Deserve. Demand.

We've talked briefly about what is at stake when our hidden vulnerabilities, our potholes, grow and crack beneath the surface. But what does that actually feel like?

Whenever someone gets close to an unacknowledged or unprocessed wound or fear, we feel a disturbance keenly within our personal ecosystems. Their nearness often triggers our defenses, even when we cognitively know the person means us no harm. Perhaps they're simply offering an observation because they care, and yet we feel attacked. Most of us have an internal dialogue that helps us process information we receive about our experiences and interactions. *How did they find that part of my story? I've worked so hard to keep it hidden, I can't let them see it. I must protect it at all costs.*

As our hiding places are disrupted, our desires for both healthy and unhealthy outlets begin stirring. This part of the process can sometimes lead us down a path of denying reality by way of storytelling. We tell stories about what we see and hear and feel all the time. Usually they are harmless, and often they're helpful. Yet sometimes we create a storyline to justify our hiding, and this may mean villainizing the person asking to be invited in. *I'm not the one in the wrong here; it's them.*

We may use these inner stories to justify other less healthy responses. If we choose to soothe ourselves by taking one of our pet distractions into hiding with us, we'll tell ourselves we've earned it. That we deserve a reward. *I've worked hard. Nobody understands what I'm going through. If anyone deserves this reward, it's me.* When these stories come scurrying down the mental track, they can be challenging to abort.

To sum up this process, someone or some circumstance shined a bit of unwelcome light on your pothole and threatened to expose hidden vulnerabilities. Your comfort was disturbed, which triggered you to seek out your desires. You justified your desires with a narrative of your own invention. And now, you demand to satisfy those desires. Anything to avoid dealing with that pothole. You're doing what you have to in order to push the offending person or circumstance away and keep your secret safe.

Much of this is subconscious, and most of the time, we are not aware of our motivations for acting this way. All we feel is what is on the surface, and that usually gets labeled things like "judgment" or "condescension." Often, in an effort to defend ourselves, we will inflict damage on other people, which only causes more internal shame and pushes us further into our hiding places. We click "buy" on that shirt that's been sitting in our cart. We eat a tub of ice cream or binge for ten hours of TV. We flirt with the stranger online, or we go out and drink too much just to make the feeling stop.

Sometimes this hiding is extreme, and other times it's very subtle. As a pastor, I'm more concerned with the silent and subtle escapes we run back to again and again. For many of us, these are socially acceptable vices that we use to deflect our attention from addressing the honest truth. Deflecting from our wounds, we begin accruing future pain as we start a process of disintegration and try to make our hurting selves invisible. But people will eventually notice our potholes, whether they manifest in a lack of connection, truth telling, or authenticity.

This is what happened in the story of King David and Bathsheba. As you may recall, David was supposed to be at war with the rest of his military. But for some reason, he chose to stay home. Yes, the most powerful man in the kingdom—if not in the world at that time—decided to sit out the fight. David wasn't where he was supposed to be, doing what he was meant to do. And it appears this disturbed him. So while he stood outside on his deck taking in the view, his eyes landed on a woman bathing. Bathsheba expected all the men to be at war. She would have assumed her king was far away as well.

David noticed her beauty, and his desire quickly turned unhealthy (2 Sam. 11:1–2). He began telling himself a story. *I deserve to have her. For I'm the king. And I'm under a lot of pressure.*

Next David ordered one of his servants to call for Bathsheba. It's important to acknowledge here that she would not have had any real choice but to obey. Although the Bible doesn't provide these details, we have every reason to believe she was forced into this situation against her will. To deny this powerful man would have meant punishment and possibly even death.

David demanded she stay, eat with him, and sleep with him. And as a result of this night together, Bathsheba became pregnant with David's child. Now she had to go back and tell him the news, fully exposing the grievous sin he'd committed (vv. 3–5). Shining a light on his secret pothole. And David was triggered.

What have we learned that we tend to do when our secrets are about to be unveiled for all to see? We hide. And David was no different.

He immediately crafted a plan to cover his tracks, which involved the death of Bathsheba's husband (vv. 14–17).

Oh, how quickly a pothole can become a sinkhole. A secret becomes a cesspool where sin festers and multiplies. Ultimately, what began as a means of protecting ourselves hurts not only us but those around us. Even a sin that goes unnamed and unacknowledged affects its environment. Sin leaks. All over us and our loved ones.

In David's case, he saw something he desired, he convinced himself he deserved it, and he demanded it. The resulting collateral damage was a movement that started as a troubling abuse of power, led to a sexual assault, and ended with a murder. In his example, we see how dangerous the progression of desire, deserve, and demand can be.

Thankfully, for most of us, our sins and our wounds—all our secret, shame-provoking places—will never lead to anything so drastic. But we're remiss if we presume we aren't negatively affecting our lives by keeping things buried, by perpetuating patterns in which we're triggered to hide and soothe and seek instant gratification rather than healing.

As we've established, no one traveling the road of life comes through unscathed. We all endure pain, betrayal, and disappointment. Some of it self-inflicted. We may have been left behind, overlooked, and underestimated. These wounds are real, and we won't simply "get over them."

Potholes don't fix themselves.

So how do we go about unearthing our deeply buried sources of shame? Where will we find courage to face the thing beneath the thing, that thing we're most afraid of? And when we discover it, what shall we do about it? How can we prepare for the next time someone trips on one of our potholes and triggers us to fight, take flight, or freeze?

Let's take a deep dive together into the places God wants to heal.

The places where we have room to grow. On the other side of our pain awaits a life of security and confidence in the One who knows us best.

My prayer is that you come to a more intimate knowledge of him as the One who loves you most.

DIG A LITTLE DEEPER

1. One of the first places we go when we are triggered is to a specific hideout where we co-opt good to escape the pain of our stories. Where do you find yourself running to when you get triggered?

2. What good thing have you recently used to escape discomfort or make you feel better about your circumstances?

3. Immediately after you run to this hideout to escape the pain, how do you feel? How do you feel an hour later? The morning after?

4. David saw a woman he desired, then told himself that he deserved her and demanded she come to his palace. Desire + Deserve + Demand. In what area of brokenness are you susceptible to following in David's footsteps?

04

WHEN IDENTITY BECOMES
INSECURITY

Yeah everybody wear the mask
but how long will it last?
—THE FUGEES, "THE MASK"

I'm reminded of your sincere faith.
—THE APOSTLE PAUL

WHEN I LEARNED I AM AN ENNEAGRAM TYPE THREE, "THE Achiever," it rang true.[1] I tend to be highly competitive, I enjoy sports of all kinds, and I celebrate when I can be part of problem-solving solutions with a team. It's fair to say that achieving success and having a measurable impact are of high value to me. I love winning! And I love setting others up to win too.

In case you're not yet familiar with it, the Enneagram is an ancient personality test that operates on a scale of nine numbers representing the nine personality types. I highly recommend doing some research and spending time getting to know your type if you haven't. The Enneagram has been an incredibly helpful relational and spiritual tool for me and many of my friends.

A few years back, toward the end of my time as lead teaching pastor at Willow Creek Community Church, I found myself in one of the most difficult seasons of my life to date. It was becoming increasingly impossible to find a path forward that didn't feel like someone was losing, which is the worst nightmare for a driven problem solver like me. I was struggling, barely eating or sleeping, weighed down by intense anxiety and deep sadness. There was little I had the power to change within my day-to-day context, yet the external expectation was for me to arrive at a way to fix things for all parties involved. I was losing hope and sinking fast.

Around this time, a friend of mine came to visit. I say friend because he's the type of guy you feel you've known all your life when you meet him for the first time. In fact, there's a strong chance you know him, too, because he tends to spend every moment he can with people. This man, Bob Goff, is a fireball of love, grace, and whimsy. Now in his early sixties, Bob has set up his remote office on Tom Sawyer Island at Disneyland. Because why not?

Bob spoke at Willow Creek, and after the service we spent time talking. I will never forget the truth he shared with me that day.

"Steve," he said simply, "which way is north?"

My first response was to point straight up, which made Bob laugh with his trademark joy. Then he reached into his pocket and pulled out a small, shiny compass. Nothing fancy, most likely something he bought for a dollar at a toy store. He placed it in the palm of his hand, opened it, and began moving it around until the needle pointed straight toward the *N*.

"Ha! There it is," he exclaimed. "There's north. That's the way forward."

He was obviously überexcited about this discovery, but I wasn't yet catching on.

"Yes," I said. "That does appear to be the way to go—if you want to go north. What am I missing? Why is this important?"

He looked at me. "Steve, we know the Bible says we need to fix our eyes on Jesus. It states that Jesus is our True North. So listen, my friend. You just keep your eyes, heart, mind, and life heading in that direction, and you're gonna be fine. Wake up each morning and head thataway, and take as many people with you as you can."

Then he handed me that golden compass, told me he was proud of me, gave me a giant bear hug, and walked out. For the next few weeks, amid even more chaos and pain, I carried that compass in my pocket like a talisman. What a comfort. Like a security blanket for a young child. Each time I reached into my pocket and turned it over and over, I remembered, *True North. Follow Jesus. Keep going thataway.*

Before walking into each difficult meeting, I'd pause to open the compass and find my True North. This had a way of grounding me in the knowledge that my only real responsibility was to fix my eyes on Jesus. Usually, this was enough to bring me into a focused place from which I could listen and speak with security and confidence. Of course, there were also times when I slipped back into my fear of failure, of not being enough. Even on a good day, one negative comment could trigger me and send me spiraling into insecure waters.

Insecurity is tricky to identify in ourselves and others because it presents as a simple lack of confidence. But you've probably noticed that it's much more complex as it plays out. Because when insecurity whispers to people that they should make themselves smaller, these people often respond to the trigger by making themselves appear larger. Someone who struggles with insecurity can act out by either powering up or by powering down. Both postures are common responses to feelings of inadequacy or fear.

While many of us become experts in hiding our not-enoughness, others lean more toward lingering in insecurity. These responses happen whenever we lose sight of our unique imago Dei, the image of God within us. Our sense of worthiness and purpose feels far away, and we forget who we are and why we're here. Whenever we lose our centering in Christ, our identity is replaced with insecurity.

One of my favorite books in the Bible is 2 Timothy. Paul wrote it as a teacher speaking to a beloved student, whom he often referred to as his spiritual son. When we read 2 Timothy, we want to keep in mind its context. At the time, Paul had received reports that Timothy was struggling with a lack of confidence, which was affecting his ability to lead. Those around him were even said to call him Timid Timothy. It is to this issue that Paul wrote, "For God has not given us a spirit of fear and timidity, but of power, love, and self-discipline" (1:7 NLT).

Often in our downward-spiraling moments of timidity and insecurity, we tell ourselves stories that just aren't true. These stories may be baseless and even ridiculously far-fetched, but when we give them credibility, they tend to take off. When we become uncomfortable with our reality, we sometimes hide. But other times we invent a story to make our circumstances more palatable. In a way, we turn into actors within our own lives.

Living Beneath a Mask

The ancient Greeks and Romans, so focused on the body and the mind, loved their gymnasiums and theaters. The Greeks invented theater and formalized it, and the Romans, in their turn, spread it throughout their empire. In every corner of their far-flung civilization, wherever Romans lived together in any number, theaters sprang up. Or down, since most of the amphitheaters were dug into the nearest convenient hillside.

Even in the ancient Near East there were theaters. King Herod the Great, who invited the Romans into Israel to secure his own throne, built a massive freestanding theater in Jerusalem.

Timothy, whom Paul was writing to, lived not in Jerusalem but in Ephesus, where there was an even larger Roman theater. This one seated twenty-five thousand people.[2] Day in and day out, actors took the stage to perform their shows. An actor in that culture was referred to as a *hupokrité*, from which we derived our familiar word *hypocrite*.

For the Romans, to be an actor was to be a hypocrite. And while this did not hold the same negative connotation it does for Americans today, some elements carry through. Essentially, acting is pretending to be someone you're not. Just as today's performers use special effects, stage makeup, and props to create illusions that help an audience disappear into the story, ancient actors wore an array of masks to help them evolve into different characters. One definition of *hupokrité* is "one who sifts under a mask." Of course, the danger comes when we attempt to do this in our real lives too. We lose ourselves when we put on masks to keep our insecurities from view.

In Ephesus, Timothy would have seen actors in costume. He likely related to the imagery of putting on a mask to portray someone different. These references would have connected with anyone in that society at the time.

Jesus himself would have been familiar with Herod's great theater in Jerusalem. He would have likely seen actors with their bags of masks. So it shouldn't surprise us that he used this vocabulary in the Gospels. Remember that he said:

> And when you pray, do not be like the *hypocrites*, for they love to pray standing in the synagogues and on the street corners to be seen by others. Truly I tell you, they have received their reward in full. But when you pray, go into your room, close the door and pray to your Father, who is unseen. Then your Father, who sees what is done in secret, will reward you. . . .
>
> When you fast, do not look somber as the *hypocrites* do, for they disfigure their faces to show others they are fasting. Truly I tell you, they have received their reward in full. But when you fast, put oil on your head and wash your face, so that it will not be obvious to others that you are fasting, but only to your Father, who is unseen; and your Father, who sees what is done in secret, will reward you. (Matt. 6:5–6, 16–18, emphasis mine)

The Greek word behind "hypocrites" in these passages is, you guessed it, *hupokritès*. "Hey," Jesus seemed to be saying, "in your real life, don't be like actors on a stage. Don't treat your life like a play or theatrical performance. Don't try to fake us out. Don't carry a bag of masks to hide behind when you feel insecure. What my Father desires is masklessness, a truly authentic life. Let me see the real you."

Jesus had long witnessed how the religious leaders, those followers of God who were supposed to be wonderful examples for the Jewish people, were acting. They were fixated on getting people to look at them and to think of them in specific ways. They weren't as interested in actually being pious, in actually manifesting holiness, as they were in having onlookers credit them with those qualities. Their lives weren't about pointing people to the goodness of the Father. Their lives were about collecting the accolades of humans. They were practicing *hupokritès*.

Yet seventeen times in Matthew 6, Jesus strongly communicated: Do not be an actor. Do not be a hypocrite. Do not be someone who wears a mask to capture the fixation and approval of the crowd. Your responsibility as you continue to learn and grow is to discern what God wants to do in and through you and to be about that work.

We face danger when we live under metaphorical masks. For one thing, we run the risk of being believed and getting in over our heads in situations where our actual level of ability or character doesn't match what our masks have promised. For another, we are never fully known. Which mask is our real face? What if it's none of them, if there is not one mask in our entire bag that depicts who we really are? And finally, we'll eventually be exposed as frauds. Those who thought they knew us, who built entire relationships on assumptions about us, may need to break ties when they realize we were something else entirely. What part of us wasn't a lie?

Even in ancient Greek and Roman culture, people saw the dangers of living too long behind a mask. Fearing an actor might forget who he really was, society warned actors not to remain in character for too long.[3] In our own culture we practice the opposite. Theater students learn about *method acting,* an approach where actors are instructed to become their characters, never stepping out of their roles for as long as the movie is being shot or the play is in production.

The late Heath Ledger was a method actor. In the movie *The Dark Knight* he fully became the Joker. While the movie was still being edited, Ledger died of an accidental overdose of prescription drugs. After his death, stories circulated about the difficulties Ledger navigated in his mind and soul as he became that violent, depraved character. His performance was widely hailed, and he became the first posthumous recipient of the Australian Film Institute International Award for Best Actor. And yet we have to wonder if he became, in too great a sense, the character he was only meant to imitate.

Living under a mask does something to us.

This idea was on Paul's heart when he thought about his young friend Timothy from a prison 830 miles away. As I mentioned earlier, Paul had a deep affinity for Timothy. "To Timothy, my dear son," he began his letter (2 Tim. 1:2).

I love that. *To Timothy, my dear son.* We don't know much about Timothy's father except that he was Greek. Many scholars believe Timothy's dad bailed pretty early in Timothy's life. We know Timothy's mother was Jewish (2 Tim. 1:5). And Timothy, being half-Greek and not circumcised, was disallowed from entering any synagogue (Acts 16:1–3). This left him kicked out of both societal groups. The Jews rejected him as a Greek Gentile, and the Greeks wouldn't receive him because they thought he was a Jew.

If you have ever felt the sting of being abandoned by a parent or other family member, you can understand what Timothy must have felt. I imagine that every day he felt the insecurities and pressures of being unwanted. Perhaps every day he wrestled with an identity crisis. *Who am I? Why am I here? What's my place?*

The first thing Paul did was address that identity crisis. *You want to know who you are, Timothy? I'll tell you. You are a permanent fixture in my heart.*

Paul continued, "I thank God, whom I serve, as my ancestors did, with a clear conscience, as night and day I constantly remember you in my prayers. Recalling your tears, I long to see you, so that I may be filled with joy. I am reminded of your sincere faith, which first lived in your grandmother Lois and in your mother Eunice and, I am persuaded, now lives in you also" (2 Tim. 1:3–5).

Let's look at this one phrase: "I am reminded of your sincere faith." The word "sincere" here is related to *hypocrite*. And it has literally the opposite meaning.

The Greek word is *anupokritos*, which is *hupokrités* with a negating prefix on the front. The *an-* prefix is similar in meaning to our prefix *anti-*. An antipersonnel mine in warfare is a weapon used against personnel. An antiseptic is used against sepsis, or infection.

Timothy's faith, according to Paul, was anti-hypocritical. Paul was saying, "I am reminded of your non-hypocritical faith, Timothy. You're no actor. You're no pretender. Your faith is sincere and authentic. It moves you to tears. And that buoys my heart even as I sit in this Roman prison far away. I saw this kind of real, honest faith in your grandmother and in your mom, and I'm persuaded it will stay with you all of your days."

Timothy was the un-hypocrite. His faith was sincere—or at least it had been once. But now Paul had heard that Timothy's faith might be wavering and in danger of becoming hypocritical. So he wrote this letter to say, "Timothy, you were made for even more. Don't let your faith become hypocritical."

This sounds simple enough, but we know how hard it is to take off the masks we've crafted to keep us safe. Especially for those of us who grew up learning to use masks to protect ourselves from the sting of feeling less than. In every business meeting, across every meal, in every conversation with friends, neighbors, and teammates, we feel tension to choose between acting and authenticity.

According to Paul, a person walking through life wearing masks is a hypocrite, and a hypocrite's faith is insincere.

How do you feel about that? As you read those words, what do you sense creeping up in your spirit? I can tell you it stirs a reaction of concern in me because it challenges me to expose areas I would rather keep hidden. It hits a little too close to home. I'm not sure I want to take off all my masks and allow you to see all of me. What if you don't like what you see?

What if you shame me?

Judge me?

Cancel me?

As a guide to help you discover your own disguises, I have identified five common masks we tend to carry: the performer, the pleaser, the perfecter, power, and the pretender. As you read through them, take notes. Pay attention to what you're experiencing internally. These responses will help you discover your personal potholes, leading to insights that will help you map out new ways to grow.

The Performer Mask

Those wearing a performer mask expect to find their identity in their achievements and successes. They love to flip a switch and be "on." They enjoy the thrill of being noticed. They base much of their value on what people think about them. When they do well, they codify that behavior into a *persona*, which is the Latin word for mask.

I learned I wore the performer mask in the fifth grade while playing four square. I was in third position and making my way to the top when Matt, the kid in the second square, got me out. I was really mad, so I backed up and got into line, while giving him the stink eye, with this "prayer" on my lips: "Dear God, please keep Matt in the game long enough for me to get him out."

I finally got back in and moved up. Matt was in the king's square, and I was a few squares away. As the game progressed, I had several chances to get other kids out, but I passed them all by. I wasn't there just to advance in the game—I was gunning for Matt. Finally, I got my chance. I turned the corner with power and authority and knocked him out. Oh, sweet victory. "Take that!" I taunted. "How's it feel, huh? That's right, step out." I felt vindicated. The universe had been fixed.

Eventually I got knocked out of the game and found myself standing by an older student I thought the world of. "Hey, Steve," he said, "it seemed like you took it really personally when Matt got you out. Why was that?"

"Because he got me out." Didn't this guy understand that my entire worth had been thrown into dispute when Matt got me out? Wasn't he proud of me for restoring the balance?

But my older friend just shook his head and walked away. And suddenly I had a glimpse of how I must have looked from an outside perspective. I couldn't put words to it yet, but on some level I saw that I believed my identity was wrapped up in how I performed. My persona, the mask I preferred, was the one that showed me as the best athlete in the class. So, of course, I took it personally when someone bested me in a sport. But now it looked petty and immature.

Do you wear the mask of performance too? Do you define your

identity in large part by your level of achievement and success? It may help to ask yourself, *What happens when I fail? What happens when I get out? What happens when someone demonstrates superiority over me in a competition? How does this make me feel? And what does it make me think about myself?*

I could've brought kindness and encouragement to a promising young athlete, but instead I couldn't see beyond my own fears, my own mask, my own hypocrisy. The older student who pulled me aside was the difference maker in that situation because he put me on the path to realizing where I was off.

This reminds me of what Paul wanted to communicate to Timothy. He wrote, in effect, "Please, son, you've got to get back to your sincere faith. Receive grace and mercy and peace, and please do not anchor your worth in your level of performance."

Sometimes when I read the Scriptures, I imagine the writer speaking those same words to me. Reminding me to ground my identity in Christ and his love for me rather than any success, achievement, or accomplished goal. I wonder what that writer might say to you. If you, too, struggle with the performer mask, I can almost guarantee the words would remind you that you are more than enough with or without the win. God knows you for who you are as his child, his beloved and cherished creation, and you are exactly and wonderfully enough as you are.

The Pleaser Mask

Those who wear the pleaser mask tend to help everyone. They even seem to know your needs before you do. If you have a need, they jump right on it.

Sounds good, right? But here's the thing about pleaser masks: the intention to help is good, but the motivation is off. In a way, this is a perversion of service. Those hiding behind a pleaser mask aren't doing something without expecting anything in return. They want to secure a favorable position in your atmosphere. All of this happens subconsciously. It's not like your neighbor is over there sitting at her dining table, scheming up ways to make you like her. But her thoughtful service may mask a subtle insecurity. And that is truly sad. It's sad for her because she's unable to trust that her true self is worthy enough for you. And it's sad for you because you're missing out on getting to know the amazing, authentic person under the mask.

People who wear the pleaser mask often fixate on solving other people's problems. They carry a heavy sense of responsibility on their shoulders to take care of everybody else, often at the expense of their own self and soul.

Perhaps you harbor an unspoken, unacknowledged belief that if you can't manage a given situation, a certain person will be unhappy. And if you can't make that person happy, you'll be excluded—from the job, from that circle of friends, from a church community, from that family group. Pleasers may not feel the need to please everyone, only certain key people or groups. Yet they may be horrified by the lines they're willing to cross (or find themselves already across) if they feel they're about to lose a key person's approval.

You can't bring your true self to the lives of others until you get rid of this disguise. You can never know the fulfillment of being authentic while wearing the pleaser mask. And you were made for more than that.

Paul was also saying, "Timothy, do not be a pleaser. If you're trying to please every person, you'll tune out what God wants to say to you and through you." When you find yourself valuing the approval of others over the purposes of Jesus Christ, your faith has lost all power. One of the greatest challenges to remember as believers is that we're called to live our lives for an audience of one, God alone. To listen and respond to what God is inviting us into. If you wrestle with people pleasing or making other voices louder than God's, ask yourself how it feels deep within your soul. I know for me, when I lose sight of my audience of one, exhaustion kicks in. The beautiful invitation that God extends to all of us recovering pleasers is to focus only on his voice as it cancels out the rest. Perhaps it's time to drop the mask, embrace a sincere faith, and accept all the love he has waiting for you.

The Perfecter Mask

The perfecter mask is preferred by the person who fears being wrong. Outwardly, this looks like someone who always has to be right. This person may constantly challenge your method or way of doing something. This may be the person in the meeting who defends their answer even when it's clearly not accurate. And when proven incorrect, this person probably turns defensive and argues that it wasn't their fault. That they didn't have all the information they needed. In this way, they can hold on to the idea that, technically, they were at least partially right, even if they were mostly wrong. Because they must be right. All. The. Time.

If this feels a little too close to home, you are absolutely not alone. I can be so stubborn when it comes to winning an argument that I lose sight of what I was even fighting for in the first place. When self-righteousness is driving this car, the motivation or fuel behind an interaction shifts from seeking to understand and connect to winning at all costs. Perhaps there has been a time in your past when you had to be the one who was seen as bright, flawless, and most of all, right. Ironically, people who wear the perfecter mask are the ones with the highest levels of self-criticism, yet this expresses as criticism of others.

The person wearing a perfecter mask usually has a hard time showing vulnerability. Perfecters believe the lie that they have to have it all together. In their family, work, and home lives, they're under constant pressure to appear perfect to the outside world. No mistakes allowed. They attach deep shame to any flaws that creep through the surface. Yet beneath a seemingly flawless outside, the perfecter is crumbling. Cracking. Breaking. Because even perfecters have potholes.

To the perfecter aspect of his young friend, Paul would say, "Timothy, please be sincere. You don't need to come across like you have it all together. Don't try to have some perfectionist kind of faith. When you live like this, what need will you have for Jesus?" The same is true for each of us. Whenever we act like we have it all together or are perfect in all we're doing, we actually are trying to box Jesus out of the conversation. This is how Paul lived his life before he encountered God's goodness and grace. From then on, he declared that if he were going to boast, it would be in his weakness because he understood that is where God does his best work (2 Cor. 12:5–10). Perfection attempts to push God away. Weakness always draws God in. My friends, when you drop the mask, you're letting more of God in, which can only add value to your already valuable life.

The Power Mask

Often with insecurity, we play ourselves as less than who we were meant to be. But another form of insecurity is pride—that consistent stubbornness that is unable to wave the white flag, surrender, and ask for help. When people who default to this mask find themselves triggered, they don't play small. They power up. With tone and energy, with threats or negativity, people who wear the power mask seek to belittle their opponents so they will quickly back down.

Fortunately, our culture is becoming more aware and better prepared to respond to serious abuses of power in the workplace, in homes, and even in churches.

Power is just a mask, an attempt to veil someone's deep insecurity and detract from personal potholes. In other words, a person who is protecting deep emotional vulnerabilities may respond to a trigger by stonewalling, shutting down, or spewing harsh words. The person may intimidate or do whatever it takes to overpower another in hopes the other person will surrender.

The emotional abuse that proceeds from the mouths of unhealthy yet powerful authority figures—leaders, parents, coaches, teachers, bosses—sticks to people. Perhaps these abusers themselves were subjected to people wearing a power mask, so now they in turn diminish the imago Dei in others. The bullied become the bullies. But it's just a disguise. And sadly, these people become shells of themselves while creating unfathomable pain in others.

These behaviors are a dramatic but all-too-common symptom of unaddressed potholes, which easily create painful emotional sinkholes for others. When you choose to drop the mask, you realize that sincerity is always better than powering up. People who power up don't actually trust their own ideas or the people they're degrading, but sincere leaders turn that energy and power they're feeling inside to unleash and empower others. This is what Paul was doing for Timothy and what each of us can do for those around us.

The Pretender Mask

When someone asks, "Hey, have you seen that movie?" the person under the pretender mask might say, "Yeah, it was awesome," even if they haven't seen it. "Yeah, that actor is so good. What was his name again? Oh, yeah, yeah. He's great. I love him."

Someone will ask, "Have you heard of this book?" and the person wearing the pretender mask will respond, "Oh, yeah, I read it. It's amazing. So good."

But pretending may have just landed that person in a load of trouble. Because now the other person might say, "Wait. How have you read it? It hasn't even come out yet."

Now the pretender is forced to keep the lie going. "Well . . . I've got a friend who's got a friend who knows someone in publishing who sent a press copy. It's awesome. So good. Hey, I've gotta run—bye!"

Why can't we say we haven't yet seen that movie or read that book or eaten at that restaurant? Why is it so hard to say, "I don't know"? Why don't we say what we mean and mean what we say? Why is it that we feel we have to pretend at all?

The person wearing the pretender mask wants to always be in and never be out. Pretenders believe their entire worth will disappear in a puff of smoke if others have more, do more, or know more. They feel a burning need to be more. Something inside them, some hidden pothole, has them thinking if they don't portray themselves as more than they truly are, they will be ostracized.

When being "in" is perceived as a matter of soul survival, no price is too high.

Andre Agassi was a tennis superstar back in the 1990s. He brought tennis into the mainstream for my generation. A style icon, Andre strutted onto the court with heaps of swagger. Gold earrings and a gold chain. Nikes with a hit of bright fuchsia before colorful shoes were a thing. Canon paid him who knows how many millions to promote a new camera called the Rebel because that's who Andre Agassi was—a rebel to the game of tennis. Canon's slogan for that marketing campaign? "Image is everything."

Andre had a long and fabulous mullet at the time. And when he would play, that hair flew around like a lion's golden mane. Did I mention it was fabulous?

Reading his autobiography, *Open*, I was stunned to learn that his iconic, flowing hair was actually a wig. This was his signature feature, and it was a mask. What do you do when "image is everything" and you're going prematurely bald? Well, if you're Andre Agassi, you put on a wig and pretend you've got a full head of hair.

Now, don't get me wrong. Nothing about Andre's hair, or lack thereof, made a bit of difference when it came to the amazing natural athlete and tennis champion he was. He could not have won all those Grand Slams if he were a pretender when it came to tennis.

However, the pretending he felt compelled to do with regard to his image did impact his performance on the court. One year, early in his career, he made it to the finals of the French Open and was expected to crush his opponent. Instead he lost in four sets. How and why? In his book, Andre explained that he was distracted by worry, fearing his wig was coming loose. He imagined it falling off in front of an international audience.[4]

Pretenders would rather deal with people saying their efforts are weak than allow themselves to be fully seen and known with all their imperfections and vulnerabilities. Paul wanted Timothy to understand the sheer importance of sincerity. When you drop the pretender mask, you will walk truly comfortable in your own skin. Pretending is always reaching, grasping, hoping that adding this false detail will finally allow you to feel "in." Included. On the inside. My friends, when you're sincere, you can proclaim that whether you know or not, whether you have seen something or not, whether you have been there or not, you are worthy of acceptance because of what Christ has graciously invited you into.

Drop the Disguises

I don't have the answer for you, but I do believe we all need to ask ourselves this extremely important question:

How might others respond to us if we took off our masks and came clean?

Much of our healing comes from being honest. Being honest with ourselves about our need to heal in the first place. Being honest with others, always letting someone else in on the process we're working through. And asking for prayer. God made us for community. We need one another to fill in the blanks for us sometimes, to show us what we're unable to see, to speak truth to our false narratives.

Honest confession is a powerful tool when it comes to filling in those potholes with something that can truly fix us. Because confessing leads to repentance, and repentance can bring us together in reconciliation. And within the beautiful space of reconciliation, we find grace.

A person under a mask is unlikely to contribute positively to others. How can we love and serve with pure, other-centered hearts when we're busy managing our images? When we're hiding behind a mask, we aren't living fully or experiencing true peace and satisfaction. Nor can we dynamically fulfill the purposes for which God created us.

Which is why Paul desperately wanted to tell Timothy, "You're enough. So be sincere. When you drop your disguises, you're able to be seen and known. Weak is the new strong. Be an anti-hypocrite, son. Do whatever it takes to live your life for an audience of one. Keep your heart, mind, eyes, and ears open to what God is stirring. Allow others to see what you're really wrestling with. This is the kind of posture where God does his best work in you and for you. Stuff the mask away."

Are you ready to discover your own masks, my friend? None of these masks are easy to part with. They are the result of our fears and the false stories we continually tell ourselves. Addressing the issues under the masks will require the work of God, quite possibly coming alongside the work of Christian counselors. It takes courage. It also takes a sort of curiosity that keeps asking and digging. But it's well worth the time, and even the potential pain, as the answers hold the keys to a more abundant and freer future. I'm not suggesting it will be easy. But I'm promising you it'll be worth it.

DIG A LITTLE DEEPER

1. When we get triggered, one of the places we quickly run to is insecurity, and from there we begin telling ourselves a false story. What insecure stories have you told yourself recently?
2. What are your top three go-to masks that you put on?
3. Can you name the pothole (painful story from your past) that has played a huge part in your mask wearing?
4. Are you more likely to power down (think you're less than) or power up (think you're better than) when you get triggered?
5. Do you fear condescension? What potholes might have caused you to feel you're not as good as those you're trying to keep up with? Play out the scenario: Would you really be ostracized if you presented your truest self?

05

———

FROM INSECURITY TO ENVY

And I've got this friend, you see who makes me feel.

—NIRVANA, "LOUNGE ACT"

Envy will rot your bones.

—KING SOLOMON

RECENTLY SARAH AND I TOOK A RISK AND PURCHASED A little cabin in the woods of northern Arizona. We'd harbored a dream for years to provide a retreat space where we can serve ministry leaders who've been wounded by personal or congregational experiences.

The cabin's structure and bones were good, but the inside needed a lot of work. From the turquoise carpet straight out of the 1980s to the retro wood paneling over the walls and ceiling, this was a fixer-upper for sure. But we could see the potential from the first moment we walked in. We imagined knocking down walls to make room for a communal kitchen. New wood floors. A fresh coat of paint on everything. The diamond was there—just in the rough.

But here's the problem. I'm not very handy. And I'm not being modest. This is just a fact. More so, every time I walk into Home Depot, I get panicky and feel inner shame. I hear internal voices telling me, *You should know this* or *You should be able to do that*. They tell me I'm weak. A failure. Waves of insecurity come over me. And for many years, I let those voices hold me back from attempting new things.

On the day Sarah and I began laying the new flooring, I recognized the similarities between what we were doing to this little house and what the Holy Spirit had been doing in me for the past two years. We'd been in full demolition mode, stripping everything away. Just as we pulled up carpet, ripped off tiles, dismantled fixtures, and opened up spaces in the cabin to let more natural light in, my heart had been experiencing a similar transformation.

I'm beginning to understand what the ancient writer King Solomon, architect of the first temple, meant when he said, "Above all else, guard your heart, for everything you do flows from it" (Prov. 4:23). With each piece of the cabin's flooring, drywall, and cabinetry I rip away, I'm asking the Lord to do the same in my heart. To continue rooting out bitterness, envy, and bias. To raze the false scaffolding of my masks and hideouts and idols.

God so kindly provides everything I need, whether it's a wise guide in an orange apron on aisle 31 or a small encouragement to keep at it. This process has helped me understand and view spiritual formation with new depth.

Despite the abuse of power that led to his birth, Solomon grew to be an incredible man. The son of David and Bathsheba, he was widely known as the wisest person in the world. It is written that David's last words to his son were, "Observe what the LORD your God requires: Walk in obedience to him, and keep his decrees and commands, his laws and regulations, as written in the Law of Moses. Do this so that you may prosper in all you do and wherever you go. . . . You are a man of wisdom" (1 Kings 2:3, 9).

As I studied Solomon's life, I was compelled by what must have happened to create such a wise, prosperous leader. His reforms and innovations were ingenious. The improvement of defense measures. The expansion of the royal court. And financial benefits in the form of more sophisticated taxation, labor drafts of Canaanites and Israelites, tributes and gifts from foreign countries, and a land and sea trading system that used the military to protect assets and trade routes.[1] It was easy to see he was brilliant. According to the Hebrew scriptures, "The king made silver and gold as plentiful in Jerusalem as stone. And valuable cedar timber was as common as the sycamore-fig trees that grow in the foothills of Judah" (2 Chron. 1:15 NLT).

The *Ancient History Encyclopedia* says that King Solomon was "also famous for his international relationships, forming alliances with other nearby powerful nations such as Egypt, Moab, Tyre, Arabia."[2] Surely, he was someone who knew how to listen well, someone who looked for the details and nuances of things, and someone who truly understood his place in the world.

But I like to imagine Solomon spending his mornings sitting on his pavilion overlooking the great city of Jerusalem. Perhaps sipping some ancient tea and people-watching. No doubt his citizens would have been engaged in the early market work of the day. There would have been noise and laughter, hustling and negotiating, the braying of livestock and clanging of pots and pans. I wonder if Solomon ever asked himself, *What motivates my people? What drives their pursuits each day? What gets them going each morning and makes them want to succeed?*

I wonder, too, what motivates you to do the things you do every day? Why do you get up, show up for work, shop for groceries, enforce screen times and bedtimes, wash the dishes, and feed the dog? Why do you fall asleep only to wake and do it all over again? What have I left between the lines in those questions? Your reasons will be personal.

Only you can answer them.

I wonder if Solomon would have said he was wired to achieve. (Perhaps he was a Type Three on the Enneagram too.) Looking at his life, it's clear he sought to fulfill every accomplishment he could. And for the most part, he did just that. So isn't it puzzling that in Ecclesiastes 4:4 he wrote, "And I saw that all toil and achievement spring from one person's envy of another. This too is meaningless, a chasing after the wind"?

Solomon was saying, "You know what drives and motivates people to succeed, to achieve—why they want to toil, why they want to work? It's envy."

What? If I stacked all Solomon accomplished, the poise he held, and the vast praise he garnered, the last thing I would expect him to say was that the driving force behind it was envy.

Envy is a negative concept to us. But I'd like to suggest that most of us have a narrow understanding of everything envy encompasses.

The Difference Between Envy and Coveting

Envy is a form of insecurity that often rears its head when we are triggered, when someone gets too close to our precious potholes. Envy is dangerous, but before we dive deeper into what envy really is, we have to understand how it intersects—yet differs—from coveting. In many ways they are first cousins, but too often we think they are identical twins.

To covet is to yearn for or long for something or someone that is not yours. Of the famous Ten Commandments Moses received from God on Mount Sinai, "Do not covet" is the only one that speaks to thought rather than deed. "You shall not covet your neighbor's house. You shall not covet your neighbor's wife, or his male or female servant, his ox or donkey, or anything that belongs to your neighbor" (Ex. 20:17).

It is an imperative against setting your desire on things that are forbidden. The seventh commandment forbids the act of adultery. This, the tenth commandment, forbids the desire for adultery. The eighth commandment forbids stealing. This commandment forbids the desire for acquisition of another's goods. In the New Testament, Jesus described the Ten Commandments as issues of the heart's desires rather than merely prohibitions against certain outward actions.[3]

"You have heard that it was said to the people long ago, 'You shall not murder, and anyone who murders will be subject to judgment.' But I tell you that anyone who is angry with a brother or sister will be subject to judgment. . . . You have heard that it was said, 'You shall not commit adultery.' But I tell you that anyone who looks at a woman lustfully has already committed adultery with her in his heart" (Matt. 5:21–22, 27–28).

So where do we see this play out in our daily lives? You'd be hard-pressed to find a more prime example than a social media platform. Social media is a perfect storm of content for us to drown in our tendency to covet. From those who post photos of their perfectly clean homes to the humblebrags of celebrities, actors, and, yes, pastors, we are bombarded with opportunities to covet what we don't have.

When did Jim get a new car? Wow! I wonder how he afforded that! Oh, look, the Smiths are off on another beach vacation—must be nice! For many of us, we covet what our neighbors have. We desire the stuff they have: the car, the position, the influence, the friendships, the experiences, and the finances.

Now, envy shares similar traits to coveting, but it is actually much darker and more dangerous than its cousin. This is because envy is a hidden motivator provoked by a deep resentment that arises from what someone else has. Where coveting is wanting what someone else has, envy turns into a rancid resentment. Our feelings of envy evoke a simmering stew of lies and anger just waiting to boil over. Envy is relentless if we give it space in our hearts and minds. It eats us from the inside out, and before we even realize it, it takes the wheel and becomes the driving force to provoke us into action.

Solomon was saying that there is danger in the why behind what we do. Our motivation is key, and he observed both for himself and his kingdom ways that envy twisted the why behind decisions big and small. Perhaps he was warning that the reason people get up to work is because they want to have a little bit more than their neighbors at the end of the day.

Research confirms this suspicion. In one Harvard study participants were asked: Would you prefer to make $50,000 and have your neighbors and those around you make $25,000 per year, or would you rather make $100,000 a year while everyone else makes $200,000?

More than 52 percent said they'd take the $50,000 because they wanted to be a little bit better than those around them. Hello, envy![4]

Solomon observed that all work, achievement, and success sprang from one person's envy of their neighbor. What Solomon would be saying to us today is that every one of us, in some degree, in some fashion, struggles and wrestles with envy. It's known as one of the seven cardinal sins, yet many of us don't talk about it. Why is this?

I'd suggest it may be because we are desensitized to how envy feels to our souls.

How do we wake up those dull and desensitized places within so we can move toward health?

The Chokehold of Scarcity

To get to the thing beneath the thing when it comes to envy, we need to better understand the concept of scarcity. Scarcity is a state of things being in short supply. In this context, it serves as a driving energy to launch us into protecting what's ours. It's the lie that tricks us into thinking there is not enough good to go around.

When we live our lives driven by scarcity, we operate as if we're in competition with others. Thus, we set ourselves up to isolate, and we struggle to trust. One of the darker sides of this perspective is that we begin to anchor our identities in what we lack instead of what we have.

Someone who is mesmerized by and fixated on scarcity can't celebrate success or good fortune for someone else. To do that would be to admit they don't view the other as a threat; to do that would be to concede that scarcity is, in fact, a myth. Sadly, because they define themselves by what they lack, their outlook on life and other people is negative and narrow. When someone else succeeds, they take it personally, as if they have lost.

Does any of this hit home for you? It's okay to admit if the answer is yes. We all experience some form of this from time to time. It's natural and in some ways hardwired into our DNA to want to do better than those around us. Survival of the fittest and all that. But is it setting you up to live the best version of your life possible? Is it satisfying your needs to be loved and secure in your value as a person beyond what you bring to the table? Do you believe that there is enough to go around, or do you define your value primarily by what you lack, neglecting what you have?

Envy has these shadow sides to it, these ulterior motives driving the why behind what is happening when envy takes over. We can also describe this as the theory of limited good. This theory centers on the belief that there is only so much good to go around, only so many blessings to be handed out, and if you want in on the action, you better hustle and cut corners to make sure you're in the receiving line.

In the ancient Near East, there was actually a popularly held belief about why one person would receive blessings while another was overlooked. It became known as the *good eye* and the *evil eye*.

Many people of the day believed that if you looked at someone, you could almost teleport your negativity and your cursing onto a person without saying it, and that would cause turmoil, death, disease, and sickness. By just staring at a person, you could actually choke out that limited good, releasing it back into the region so that it could be equally distributed to everyone. The stink eye, the eye roll, the glare, and the death stare are all modern-day versions of this. To my fellow parents, I know you feel me.

Back then, people started making jewelry to protect themselves against the evil eye, and the design is still around today. In fact, odds are you've seen these bracelets, a small eye with little crystals called amulets. I was in the Middle East last year and saw a number of people walking around with them, trying to protect themselves from the envy of others.

In her wonderful novel *The Language of Flowers*, Vanessa Diffenbaugh built a story around a floral chart that attributed meaning to different varieties of flowers. The most familiar of these flowers was the red rose, to which we attribute the idea of true romantic love.

Curious if there was a flower to symbolize envy, I did some research and came to find that blackberry plants have been used to represent envy, arrogance, sorrow, and haste. Blackberry plants are notorious for being brambly and wild, with large vines and twisting thorns. They tend to take over whatever patch of land they are planted in and are considered a nuisance to many gardeners. Not unlike envy itself, a blackberry bush will literally choke out the life of its host and surroundings.[5]

This is exactly what insecurity looks like when it takes the form of envy in me. It attempts to choke out the good within another, but it ultimately succeeds in choking out the joy and goodness in me.

Why Not Me, God?

Here's one strong indication you are on a path to entertaining envy. You hear yourself utter the words, "It's just not fair." When we start whispering and ruminating on sentiments like these, we transform insecurity and envy into false injustice. This alternate reality serves as justification for our subsequent self-righteous behaviors.

Think about gossip. Whenever we engage in gossiping about another person, we are, in essence, working to put them back in their place. It's scattering seeds of untruth that risk taking root and choking out the good in someone, simply because you aren't so sure you're as good and loved and okay as they are. Gossip is a clue that you're suffering from a form of insecurity manifesting as envy.

So we have insecurity.

Insecurity that leads to envy.

And envy that leads to a fear of scarcity.

Which buys into the theory of limited good.

And once we succumb to the lie that there isn't enough to go around, we make ourselves the victim. We fall into the trap of entitlement.

Because, why not me?

Insecurity dressed in envy will always make you ask, *Why are they getting what they want while I'm still doing without?*

Why don't I deserve the good?

Why don't I deserve the promotion?

Why don't I deserve a happy marriage?

Why don't I deserve a salary increase?

Why don't I deserve it?

Why not me?

Entitlement pushes into our insecurities and whispers lies. *I deserve this good thing and they don't. I deserve it because I'm better than them. I followed the rules, subscribed to the right theology, attended the right schools, landed the right job, moved to the right neighborhood . . . and they didn't do any of that, so why don't they just pull themselves up by their bootstraps and get to work?*

No cutsies in line, after all.

Whenever I see this playing out in myself or another, I realize that beneath our why-not-me questions is an important but un-acknowledged word—and the real question we're wrestling with: Why not me, God?

And this is why we don't often want to talk about envy; when we get deep, deep down there to the actual thing beneath the thing, we dis-cover our raw frustration with God. Why did God bless them and not me? Why, God, is it so easy for them to get pregnant and not me? Why, God, did he get promoted instead of me? Why, God, are they always off on some tropical vacation while I'm stuck working this low-rate job to make ends meet? Why, God, does that person have the abilities, strengths, and opportunities they do?

Why, God, why?

When these questions are right there, typed out in front of our eyes, they seem extreme and childish. But if we're honest, don't we have a stream of similar thoughts running through our minds all too often? Again, social media is a natural conduit for envy because the triggers keep coming at us. And it's so easy to write off someone's success in order to comfort ourselves. *It must be so easy for them, but I deserve it more.* (Why, God?) For me personally, this is one place in my life where I often notice envy creeping up.

"Envy," Solomon wrote in his book of wisdom, "rots the bones" (Prov. 14:30).

It will rob you of satisfaction.

Steal your joy.

Eat you alive from the inside out.

Envy is also a taboo topic, an emotion we assign shame to because it seems so weak. We're above all that, right? Sure. Sure we are. Perhaps on the surface we are. But underneath all our bravado and promise of confidence is a river of insecurity. A lifetime of wounds that have taught us how it feels not to be able to count on love. That is what is driving our fear of not being enough.

Unless we're invited into a safe space to talk about the thing beneath the thing openly, we will forever keep it hidden. We'll keep our questions to ourselves. And instead of letting it out into the light so we can be free of it, we will use our pain as fuel to hurt others.

We'll give the evil eye.

We'll gossip.

We'll slander.

Out of our triggered insecurity, we'll bring others down.

Friends, it's hard to be a human. Especially in today's world, where our every move is accessible and our every word is dissected, it's nearly impossible not to mess up in the public arena. And in an effort to secure our place in this strange world, we can be quick to jump all over someone else who fails out in the open for all to see.

This is cancel culture. And it prevents us from learning together, imperfectly, with grace. You and I are going to have to check our entitlement, our doctrine of scarcity, our envy, and our insecurity before we tear someone down for not being perfect. As if we are.

If you'll allow me to vote for the one person on earth who had good reason to feel insecure, I'm going to go ahead and say it was the brother of Jesus. I mean, can you imagine being compared to the one guy who was literally perfect? Talk about sibling rivalry.

Yet in the book he contributed to our New Testament, James wrote these words: "For where you have envy and selfish ambition, there you find disorder and every evil practice" (James 3:16). Wherever envy exists, it turns order into chaos and leads to evil (which, you'll recall, is simply co-opted good).

Then a few verses later James wrote, "What causes fights and quarrels among you? Don't they come from your desires that battle within you?" (4:1).

I imagine James didn't say those words lightly. I'll bet he often had to wrestle envy to the ground. Instead of living by the code and theory of limited good, he had to choose to see and celebrate the good and believe there was more than enough to go around.

More Than Enough

Envy teaches us that there are no free refills. But God's goodness is the ultimate free refill! There is more than enough goodness, favor, and grace to go around. We only have to choose to see it and receive it.

As we return to what Solomon had to say about envy, we read, "Better to have one handful with quietness than two handfuls with hard work and chasing the wind" (Eccl. 4:6 NLT). I love this. Solomon's wisdom teaches us that the most whole, holy, and spiritually healthy people he encountered were those who learned to be content with the peace, rest, and satisfaction of enjoying what they already had. His ultimate wisdom tells us not to waste our lives focusing beyond the good that's right in front of us or making sure we have more than anyone else.

I'd like you to do this with me for a moment: Hold out one hand in front of you. Open it, palm up. Now look. Take a deep breath and name five things you're thankful for right now. They can be big or small, ordinary or extraordinary. No need to humblebrag either. If you recently succeeded at something, say that. If you made it another day without drinking, say that. Perhaps it's the clean drinking water in your glass or the freshly laundered clothes piled up on your couch or simply the fact that you have a couch at all. You can be thankful for anything, as long as you slow yourself down long enough to allow the sensation of gratitude to wash over you.

Because if what Solomon said is true, while one hand holds your gratitude, the other is wide open to what God wants to do with you, through you, in you, and for you. That hand can celebrate someone else's victories with a high five. And it can reach out and bless another, serve another, pray for another. If the man who pretty much had it all, saw it all, did it all proclaimed that it's better to have less but be grateful, then perhaps we should pay attention to that.

Insecurity is no way for you to live, and you don't have to. There is more than enough of God's goodness to go around.

DIG A LITTLE DEEPER

1. When someone gets close to our potholes and we get triggered, envy often rushes in as a result of our insecurity. Where are you struggling with scarcity (the theory of limited good) in your life right now?
2. Who do you envy and why?
3. Do you ever wrestle with the thought that God is holding back on blessing you? In what areas of your life do you wrestle with this?
4. What good has God brought forth into your life that you need to thank him for?
5. What would it feel like for you to take Solomon's wisdom seriously in your own life this week? What are some practical ways you can lean into your insecurities and learn to release them rather than react to them with fear?

BIASES THAT DRIVE NARRATIVES

*What a sad era when it is easier to
smash an atom than a prejudice.*

—ALBERT EINSTEIN

Do everything in love.

—THE APOSTLE PAUL, 1 CORINTHIANS 16:14

I ENTERED THE LARGE AUDITORIUM IN RURAL INDIANA
where I was scheduled to speak and found myself in the middle of what
sounded like a riot. Two large groups of students were shouting back
and forth at each other—a fight seemed likely to break out. This was a
Christian camp, but I was still pretty nervous.

Walking closer to the action, I was able to discern that one group of
students was chanting "Boiler up!" then clapping twice in unison and
screaming louder, "Boiler up!" It took me a second, but I soon realized
this was the Purdue University chant (and these were the first true
Purdue fans I had ever seen in the wild).

All the while, from the other side of the room students chanted
back, "We're IU! We're IU!" in reference to the Hoosiers of Indiana
University. The Purdue fans had way more passion and moxie, but
nothing seemed to faze the IU fans. They acted as if they were merely
trying to antagonize an annoying little brother. Still, what began as
friendly jesting was quickly becoming more intense, with taunts and
chants turning personal, bordering on cruel.

I stood by the door watching it all unfold, trying to discern how
best to address these kids. The camp host was up first. He went
onstage and managed to somewhat calm everyone down. After a few
announcements and worship songs, I walked onstage to deliver the
sermon I had prepared several days earlier. But watching these fellow

students scream and sling their insults at one another across the aisle had given me a new idea, so I tossed my original plan. Instead, I drew an imaginary line down the middle of the stage. I invited those who were Purdue fans to come up and stand on one side of the line and all the IU fans to stand on the other. That left the seats in the auditorium basically empty, aside from a handful of Notre Dame and Butler fans who were faithfully staying put.

I asked both sides to choose a student to serve as a representative of their preferred school. After a quick deliberation, two brave kids stepped forward, looking a little nervous about suddenly bearing the weight of responsibility to speak for all the others. Before any more trash talk could begin, I stood between them, one foot on each side of the line, and asked them to share why they believed their school was head and shoulders above their rival.

The Purdue fan went first. "We developed quarterbacks like Bob Griese, Jim Everett, Len Dawson, Drew Brees, and Kyle Orton. We are a quarterback factory." (I thought Kyle Orton was a stretch, but I loved the confidence.) All the Purdue fans cheered and resumed their "Boiler up" chant.

The IU fan shook his head and replied, "We have Assembly Hall, the best warm-ups in college basketball, and we had Isiah Thomas, Calbert Cheaney, Steve Alford, and the greatest coach ever, Bobby Knight!" The IU fans lost their minds when Bobby Knight was mentioned. (Had they forgotten he choked a player and threw a chair on the court after a third foul was called against IU in less than a minute?)

Next, I asked the Purdue fan, "What is one thing you respect about IU?" For a minute he went silent. All activity in the whole place came to a stop, with everyone on the edges of their seats, waiting to hear the reply. This kid started to tear up and uttered these words. "My grandparents raised me, and my grandfather is my hero. A few years ago he was diagnosed with cancer and it didn't look good. The doctors in our hometown said they'd done everything they could but he needed to go to the IU Health University Hospital to get the best care in the state. After four months at the hospital my grandfather was released. I'm grateful because they saved his life."

Aside from a few sniffles, you could have heard a pin drop in that vast auditorium. His story had clearly struck a chord.

Next, I looked at the IU fan and asked the same question. He stood there thinking for a second, until someone from the Purdue side yelled out, "Where are you going to school next year?" The IU fan put his head down and then blurted, "I want to be an engineer. Purdue has the best engineering program in the state and is among the best in the whole country. They gave me an incredible scholarship, so I've decided to take my talents to West Lafayette!"

I'll never forget the moment those two rivals reached across the divide and embraced. The room erupted with clapping. It was truly a made-for-TV moment. But what I couldn't get over was how God had used this as an opportunity to transform differences into a bridge. Before they took the stage, they'd only been able to tell one biased story—what separated them. But through a simple conversation, they were now able to see the humanity in each other.

What Happened to the Dream?

As I type these words, peaceful (as well as not-so-peaceful) protests have been going on for more than twenty straight days in response to the murder of George Floyd. Individuals of all ethnicities and social demographics are proclaiming that Black lives matter and standing up for their neighbors like never before. Even people who have not personally experienced racism are waking up to its prevalence. They are buying books by minority authors, subscribing to podcasts on race and intersectionality, asking for governmental reforms, and calling out racial bias. This awakening isn't only taking place in the United States but throughout the entire world. In homes everywhere, the unjust trauma experienced by the Black community for over four hundred years is front and center in our nightly discussions.

As a little kid, I'd sometimes sneak into my dad's office and dig through his old records. I'm talking dozens of milk crates stuffed with all manner of musical genres. The Beatles; Led Zeppelin; Creedence Clearwater Revival; Earth, Wind & Fire; Joni Mitchell; Jimi Hendrix. You name it, he had it. And I loved it. This was like a hidden peek into a part of my dad I didn't know very well. He had been a film student at USC and was a bit of a hippie before he settled down into a respectable nine-to-five job. I would run my hand along the open edges of the album covers, always careful not to bend or scratch a single thing. Funny how small things can make such an impact on our memories.

A few years ago, I drove up to Michigan to visit with him. On oxygen almost constantly by this time, Dad was pretty frail due to years of struggle after having survived leukemia and enduring a bone marrow transplant. Even still, one evening he insisted we make our way downstairs to his office after dinner. Slowly we walked down the stairway that led to the basement. He was winded from the descent and sat down on a nearby couch, motioning for me to open the closet door. From there he asked me to grab a cardboard box with "tunes" scribbled on the side in a faded magic marker. I brought it over and sat it at his feet, then came and sat beside him.

He looked at me and smiled huge. "You know I've always known about your little secret expeditions into my albums, right?"

No. In fact, I had always thought naively that this was something

I'd kept secret. Of course, as a child, I hadn't understood the notion of organizing things in alphabetical order. Ha! These days, I like to imagine my dad coming in the next morning, pulling out his crate of records, and noticing a curious hand had "rearranged" them for him. He had never let on that he knew what I was up to, and I like to think it gave him a laugh. Just as it would make me laugh if my son did that to me now.

As Dad and I sifted through the records together that day, I found *Hotter Than July* by Stevie Wonder, which came out in 1980. As I pulled the sleeve from the cover, I noticed that the sleeve itself was quite fascinating.

On it was a picture of Dr. Martin Luther King Jr. alongside the following words:

It is believed that for a man to lay down his life for the love of others is the supreme sacrifice. Jesus Christ by his own example showed us that there is no greater love. For nearly two thousand years now we have been striving to have the strength to follow that example. Martin Luther King was a man who had that strength. He showed us, non-violently, a better way of life, a way of mutual respect, helping us to avoid much bitter confrontation and inevitable bloodshed. We still have a long road to travel until we reach the world that was his dream. We in the United States must not forget either his supreme sacrifice or that dream.

I and a growing number of people believe that it is time for our country to adopt legislation that will make January 15, Martin Luther King's birthday, a national holiday, both in recognition of what he achieved and as a reminder of the distance which still has to be traveled.

Join me in the observance of January 15, 1981 as a national holiday.

Stevland Morris, a/k/a Stevie Wonder

Wow. Every word was powerful, and I remember both of us sitting in silence for a moment after I'd read it aloud. I hadn't realized that it wasn't until 1983 that legislation was passed, and it wasn't until 1986 that Martin Luther King Jr. Day was declared a national holiday. What's more, it wasn't until 2000 that all fifty states recognized it as a national holiday. For the first decade of the new millennium, many institutions, businesses, and organizations still did not set aside the day as a holiday.

As I've considered all the reasons why this was the case, I've concluded that maybe Stevie was right. We still have a long road to travel to accomplish Martin Luther King Jr.'s dream.

Do you share that dream?

It's been several years since the day I sat with my father in his basement, reading those words. But lately I've been stirred by all the current events swirling around race and justice to dive back into some of the hard questions Stevie's note presents. What prevents us from actually taking that journey, finishing that race, and achieving MLK's dream? This is a complex conversation, one that requires care and intention to ensure we remain open enough to learn, humble enough to be wrong, and willing to use our voices to speak up and out when needed.

The layers of racism run deep. So I'll choose just a few pieces of the puzzle to unpack together here.

First, there's the element of bias. We all have biases, and most can be sorted into one of two categories: explicit and implicit. Explicit bias can be defined as an attitude or stereotype that affects our understanding, actions, and decisions in a conscious manner that we willfully choose. Essentially, this is what happens when we engage in any overt type of stereotyping, prejudice, or act of racism. Explicit bias is easier to identify and condemn than implicit bias.

It is within the second type of bias that we commonly run into trouble. Implicit bias relates to the attitudes or stereotypes we subconsciously hold that affect our understanding, actions, and decisions. The ones we're unaware of. Friends, every one of us has implicit biases. If right now you're noticing a defensive feeling rising within, that's okay. None of us wants to admit we harbor prejudices. But the truth is, simply based on being a human in this world, none of us escapes this reality.

Not Just a Few Bad Apples

While I was still living in California, my friend Andy and I went to tour the newly rehoused Holocaust Museum in Los Angeles. We joined a group of about fifty people in the lobby area and waited for our assigned guide to meet us and begin the tour. After a few minutes, an older gentleman in a sweater vest and freshly shined shoes made his way to the center of the room and introduced himself. And he asked us all to consider a question.

"Before we start this tour through our new Holocaust museum," he began, "I want to ask a simple question. Do you know what your own personal biases are? Do any of you prefer one race over another or practice any stereotyping, prejudice, or racism in your life? If you answer yes to any of this, please make your way through door number one. If not, go ahead and walk through door two."

Everyone except my friend and I quickly shuffled through door number two. We sort of stood there for a few seconds, looking at each other. We had just been having a conversation on the drive over about the ways our prejudices affect us even when we're unaware, and now this seemed like some sort of reckoning. I was sure I was overthinking it, but I couldn't be 100 percent sure that I didn't harbor bias of any kind. At the same time, neither of us wanted to look like the real jerks—in the Holocaust Museum, of all places. Thankfully, the guide came to our rescue. We walked through door number one with him and were surprised to find the rest of the group waiting on the other side.

The tour guide continued. "We all, in fact, have bias. It is much more dangerous to deny or pretend you do not than risk looking bad and admitting the truth. We cannot fix what we cannot name. The Holocaust was not caused by a few bad apples, it was enabled by the thousands who preferred to pretend it wasn't happening at all."

Wow.

I have to think it was more than just the solemn nature of the topic at hand that kept our group quiet and introspective for the remainder of the tour. I know I personally left changed, and I'm pretty sure I wasn't the only one.

Here is another way to dive into this conversation together. Did you know there was a study on implicit bias conducted with eBay ads? Back when iPods were the hot thing to have, they were a major selling item for the eBay platform. Researchers created a study whereby they tested two types of ad photos. The first showed a White hand holding an iPod, and the second showed a Black hand holding the same iPod in the same exact way. Which do you think did a better job of selling the product?

You guessed it: the ad with the White hand holding the iPod received 21 percent more offers than the one featuring the Black hand. Why was this? Explicit bias, maybe. Implicit bias, absolutely.[1]

And there's plenty more data where that came from. One study conducted by a University of Pennsylvania professor and a Cornell University graduate examined more than six hundred thousand observations of foul calls in NBA games between 1991 and 2003. Taking care to sort out a large number of non-race-related factors in calls made by referees, the researchers found that White referees called fouls at a greater rate (4.5 percent) against Black players than against White players. They also found a corresponding bias in which Black referees called more fouls against White players than Black players, although the bias was slightly less strong. This is how bias, on all sides, plays out.[2]

According to *Physician's Weekly*, researchers examined data from fourteen previously published studies of pain management in American emergency rooms (ERs) that altogether included 7,070 White patients, 1,538 Hispanic patients, and 3,125 Black patients.

Compared to White patients, Black patients were 40 percent less likely to receive medication to ease acute pain, and Hispanic patients were 25 percent less likely, the analysis found.[3] It had been known for years that this pattern of medical treatment disparity held true. This was just the first time it was established to also be true among children.[4]

In another study, over 6,500 professors from some of the top US colleges and institutions were asked research advice via email from a fictional student. The study found that when the request for help was sent by a name generally identified with White males, there was a 25 percent increase in response compared to requests sent by names that were generally recognized as belonging to a female minority student.[5]

And You Will Be My Witnesses

Biases are alive and well, my friends, and if we are going to be able to move into the kingdom Jesus proclaimed, we must have a bias cleanse. Acts 1:8 captures Jesus' words as follows: "You will receive power when the Holy Spirit comes on you; and you will be my witnesses in Jerusalem, and in all Judea and Samaria, and to the ends of the earth."

It's helpful to view this passage within the context of the time when Jesus first spoke those words. A first-century disciple of Jesus would have understood Jerusalem as the most familiar city reference. Consider for a moment your own hometown. The place you could navigate like the back of your hand. No surprises there; just good old comfort food for the soul. Jesus told his disciples that the Spirit of God was going to come on them and change things up. The things they thought they knew had now been made new. Different. And ever expanding. From Jerusalem to the ends of the earth.

From your hometown to a spot on the map half a world away.

What happens when we travel to a new place? If we're lucky, we get to experience a bit of culture shock. We get to know how people in a different place live their lives differently than we do. Languages are different in Paris than they are in Houston. The tradition and currency and food and history—all of these are different. Of course, traveling also has the power to expose some parts of ourselves that are uncomfortable with change. Travel can show us where we have to grow, if we let it.

Jesus was giving his friends a strong heads-up in this passage. Yes, it was a beautiful and powerful proclamation of good things to come, but it also meant they were going to have to get used to change and live outside their comfort zones. Judea was full of people who were viewed as less civilized by Jerusalem dwellers. These were the people on the wrong side of the tracks, with less access to proper education, health care, opportunity, and hope. Think about this. Envision a place in your own world that fits this description.

We have places like this all over the United States, of course. More often than not, they are neighborhoods made up of an overwhelming majority of minority and low-income folks. And that didn't happen by chance.

I want you to see the similarities in the ways we tend to subtly dehumanize others, just as the disciples of Jesus would have done with *those people* in Judea. *We don't go over there or associate with them. We have no reason to try to understand them.*

I'll never forget an experience I once had standing in the TSA line. As I waited to catch my flight, a Hispanic man a few spots ahead of me was pulled from the line and made to answer a litany of questions by a condescending, blatantly racist TSA worker. I found it hard to watch this man being made to feel less than right in front of us. And more so, to know that he had to stand there and take it or face an even more dubious abuse of power. Aside from reporting the worker, which I did, I wasn't sure what more could be done.

Jesus' promise that the Spirit of God would give the disciples power was like him announcing a great cosmic bias cleanse. Just your average, everyday sort of thing to say, right? No, of course not. Please don't miss this mind-blowing bit of information. Jesus acknowledged, preemptively, that his friends and disciples were going to have a hard time not judging the new people he was asking them to interact with. He was sending them a Helper to empower and educate them. To reveal where they needed to grow. And to show them how to do just that. All those traditionally held barriers would be removed so that they might bear witness to the all-encompassing, grace-saturated love of God that was meant for everyone.

So now I have to ask you a hard question: Who are the people you look down on? Sometimes the easiest way to discover this is to place yourself in a situation that makes you uncomfortable. Instead of grocery shopping at your usual store this week, seek out a minority-owned shop and go there instead. What would happen if you drove home from work a different way, one that took you through some of the poorer neighborhoods in town? Underneath much of our resistance to these little bias-training practices is fear.

We are afraid of what we do not understand.

Why don't they dress like me? Speak like me? I believe my way is better.

It's important we stretch ourselves and work to remove these biases because Jesus said clearly he wasn't stopping at Judea. Oh no, that was just the beginning of what he had planned. Beyond Judea and those who were often categorized as the less-thans were the people of Samaria. You remember the story Jesus told about the Good Samaritan, a man from the town of . . . right. Samaria. A place everyone considered to be on the total wrong side of the tracks.

The reason he chose to use a Samaritan as the hero of the story was because no one would have seen it coming. Samaritans were hated not only because they were poor and uneducated but because they were half-Gentile and half-Jewish. They were considered impure and backward. Stories swirled, portraying them as lawless and cruel and better left isolated from the rest of society. That was the view held by most Jews of that day.

Jesus was the best at surprise takeaways. When he tossed that little gem into his proclamation, he knew it would trigger a reaction from the crowd. They would have been thinking two things. First, they would have internally rolled their eyes. *Yeah right, Jesus.* And second, those who had been following Jesus for a while would have heard an echo in his words. They would have remembered the lesson he taught them about not judging by appearances. How the Samaritan was the one who had compassion. The least likely had become the most loving. Gotta love a good plot twist like that.

When it comes to your news, are you a CNN fan or a Fox-all-the-way person? And tell me honestly, how do you feel about a person who prefers the opposite channel for their nightly national updates? Yep, I'm going there. And why not? If we're all here because we want to get to the thing beneath the thing, we must go there.

All the way there.

What about being LGBTQ+ affirming versus not allowing gay people to attend your churches, patronize your restaurants, work in your offices? How do you feel about someone who had an abortion? Or who plans to vote Democratic in a coming election? What if they're extremely rich and elitist, or perilously poor? What if you meet someone with dark skin who calls God by the name Allah?

For Jesus and his followers, where does the buck stop when it comes to grace?

To the Ends of the Earth

Where does the buck stop for you? For me, it's those Packers fans. (I kid, but the struggle is real!)

Jesus said the Spirit of God would come on you in power and you would be his witness. Not just to the people who look like you, live like you, vote like you. And not just to the ones you look down on but even to those whose ideology you fundamentally can't stand. He could have left it at that, let us humans just sit with that for a while, trying to sort out how on earth we are supposed to remove our implicit biases. But nope. Jesus wasn't done yet. He added for good measure that we should take this good news to the ends of the earth. And a first-century disciple would have understood the phrase "ends of the earth" to mean "the other." As in, a person we don't need to understand or agree with.

I'm watching this play out as racial protests continue, in the social media posts of some church leaders who refuse to even touch the conversation. Instead they toss out a blanket "All lives matter" and try to let that be enough. As I type this, it's Father's Day. This morning my wife wrote in my card, "I'm going to just go ahead and declare this All

Parents Day because all parents matter." She was kidding, of course. But she was also making a point. Of course, all parents matter, but that doesn't mean we shouldn't set aside the space to make a big deal about our dads. When we say dads matter, it doesn't imply that moms matter any less.

And when we say all lives matter, we are missing our opportunity to agree that before we can say all lives matter, Black lives must matter equally.

As Christians, we need to be able to make room for Black lives to matter too. Because for more than four centuries, most areas of our society suggested the opposite. Sadly, churches have historically been right at the top of this problem, as most leadership opportunities do not accurately reflect the demographics of their cities. As the church, we fail our world when we elect out of these most difficult conversations.

The Spirit of God is going to come on you with power and give you a bias cleanse, so you can bear witness to what God is doing in you, and in Judea and Samaria, and what he wants to do unto the ends of the earth.

You Will Receive Power

The truth of the matter is that heaven is going to be multicultural—a transcendent and beautiful reality of existing with God in the fullness of his love. But since we live in the not yet as well as the now, we can treat each day as practice for heaven.

Every person you encounter is an opportunity to live with love, grace, and peace. To be as biased toward love as our God is, to search for the good in others, and to refuse to allow our fears to become barriers that keep us disconnected.

So, friends, how do we actually do this?

We probably all agree this sounds great. And discovering ways to break through our biases can actually be boiled down to a fairly simple recipe. But if we're honest, we know how really, really hard it is to live this way every day. So let's begin with some basic understandings.

Breaking through our biases begins with self-awareness. We must be in tune with what is happening internally when we encounter others throughout our day. Not only those we meet in person but those we read about, tweet to, and like on Instagram. Who gets under your skin? Whose opinion do you have a hard time walking away from? Make an effort to notice when you feel irritated. Get curious about the why behind it.

Sometimes we don't necessarily become upset by a situation outside our comfort zone; we just feel unsafe. Our insecurities arise when we're around a person who looks or talks a certain way.

As we become aware of our implicit biases, the natural progression will be a movement toward the other. Our hearts will soften. We will make room to be wrong, to learn, and to expand our perspectives. As this happens, our hearts will begin to bend toward the very person we initially built walls against. We start to see their humanity, their context, and perhaps what led them to the place and person they are.

For example, I know a number of people who are aware of the fact that Syria has been caught in a civil war since 2011, but they haven't invested any of their time, gifts, or resources to partner with the people who would most benefit from their advocacy. As we open our eyes to issues of injustice, we can't unsee what we've seen. There is no going back without compromising our spiritual conscience. And our wellness is wrapped up in theirs; my joy and hope are connected to yours. The truth is, if we make it, I make it.

We are linked together as humanity on a divine level that makes it impossible to act without effect. That is the beauty of God's economy. When Jesus says the ends of the earth, he means it. Learn to invest in the stories of people who are different from you. It matters to God!

God is already actively inviting you. Step out of your current comfort zone. You may even have a sense of what you're being asked to do. What is keeping you from getting curious about your stubborn hesitations? What is the thing beneath the thing standing in the way of you jumping up and shouting yes? Allow the Spirit to prod around in those vulnerable places.

But keep yourself guarded from shame. When we dig down, we all will find some biases. Shame only serves to shut us down. It's okay to name your biases. It's okay to discover you're a little bit racist. Just don't stay in that mental, emotional, and spiritual place. The only way to move into an anti-racist posture is to stop pretending and do the work to change. We can't do that if we're still acting like we don't have a problem.

Jesus promised us his Spirit, and the Spirit of God comes to us with power. Power to wipe away prejudices. Power to shape hearts. Power to embrace awareness, invest in others, and carry his love to the ends of the earth.

I saw on the news recently that in Central Park, an avid bird-watcher, who happened to be a Black man, crossed paths with a woman walking her dog without a leash. Knowing that off-leash dogs would scare the birds away, the bird-watcher asked the woman to follow the rules and keep her dog on a leash. When the woman chose not to, the bird-watcher pulled out his phone and began recording. What happened next underscores how far we still have to go when it comes to the racial divide.

The woman brought out her own phone. "I'm taking a picture and calling the cops," she said. "I'm going to tell them there's an African American man threatening my life."

She then asked the police to immediately send officers because she felt threatened by a Black man. Threatened by a bird-watcher? Or would it be more accurate to say she was *triggered*? And when she was triggered, she reacted by creating a narrative driven by her subconscious bias. It's fair to say she reached in her purse and pulled out her power mask and wielded it against a nonviolent bird-watcher in Central Park.

When you get triggered by someone from the other side of the tracks, or someone of a different religion or political party, what stories do you create?

Which people group are you most likely to direct your angst toward when you're triggered?

Who in your life do you see as less than?

Who in your life can't you stand?

Who in your life do you have no desire to understand?

If we're ever going to be Jesus' witness, fueled by the Spirit's power to the ends of the earth, we may need to implement a whole new operating system. Especially when we find ourselves triggered.

Thanks be to God there is a better way.

DIG A LITTLE DEEPER

1. When someone gets close to your pothole and you get triggered, often one of the first places we go is to create false narratives about other people. When have you unfairly created a false story about another person or people group?

2. Who in your life do you feel is less than (Judea)?

3. Who in your life is someone that you just can't stand? (Samaria + Ohio State)

4. Who in your life is someone that you have no desire to understand? (Ends of the earth)

5. How are you currently missing out on more of the Holy Spirit's power and preparing your heart and mind for our eternal homeland? (New Jerusalem)

Personal biases are such an important and timely topic that I think we need to spend a little more time digging down even deeper to discover our own preconceived notions. These often carry shame, but don't let that trip you up. They come with being human. And if recognized and dealt with properly, they can be powerful change agents in your life and in the world around you.

6. Think back to the last story in this chapter of the bird-watcher in Central Park. Have you ever witnessed such racial injustice? Do you remember how it caused you to feel, think, and respond?

7. What are the taboo topics for you? Syria? Immigration? Abortion? Racism? The death penalty? Access to guns? LGBTQ+ issues?

Will you go on this far-flung journey with God? Will you boldly carry the good news alongside the Creator of all? That's the question we each have to wrestle with. Will you stay safe within your familiar comfort zone or be obedient and accept the Spirit of God's invitation into greater levels of trust and dependency on him?

Writing about these emotions and experiences in a journal is a foolproof way to gain perspective and notice patterns of thought we may otherwise be oblivious to. I always begin with that. Sometimes I surprise myself with what I discover as I let myself freely write for a few minutes. Then I take time to pray about what comes up, inviting God to reveal areas in need of work and redirection.

I have to come to this practice with humility because it is hard to hear where I'm wrong. In my flesh, I would prefer the easier route, skipping this part—this deeper work. My tendency is to want to simply move ahead in life without ever really questioning why I feel certain things about a person. But it's important work. You need it, but our world also needs you to do this.

PART THREE

LIVING WHOLE, HOLY, AND

SPIRITUALLY HEALTHY

07

LET GRACE FIND YOU

Hold your mistake up.
—ARCADE FIRE, "WAKE UP"

Brother Saul . . .
—ANANIAS, ACTS 9:17

ANOTHER DAY OF HIGH SCHOOL. ANOTHER ZIT.

When I was a freshman, my face started to break out with a few zits here and there. Image was a huge deal at my Southern California high school, so every time I had to walk into the classroom with red marks on my face felt like torture. I was sure everyone was staring and whispering about my face. Looking back, they probably weren't. But we tend to assume this, don't we? All that to say, acne was not going to be cool with me. I had to find a way to get rid of it, and fast.

I got serious about skin care and asked my mom to buy me some high-quality face wash. When that didn't do the trick, I researched the best acne products. I needed something that would take my acne away once and for all. The good stuff.

While researching various acne medications, I discovered a new product that was showing tremendous results in clearing up extreme breakouts. The early findings of this drug, Accutane, were quite remarkable. But there was one hang-up. A small percentage of people taking it slipped into depression and even became at risk for suicide. Despite the risks, my mind was made up. I was going to be one of the faces in the "after" section of the Accutane ad. Not the "before." From that point on, I wanted Accutane. I needed Accutane.

I grabbed the phone book (remember those?) and searched the yellow pages for local dermatologists. I began calling medical offices, asking if they prescribed the drug for acute acne cases. I heard a lot of noes, but that didn't deter me. I knew this was the solution for my problem. Somewhere out there was a doctor who could help me. Fast forward to the *C* section of the phone book. Three rings and a receptionist transfer later, I was speaking with Dr. Catano, who agreed to have me come in for a consultation but made no promises.

"So, you're saying there's a chance!" I said. Yes, I was desperate.

I came prepared the following week and sat down in the waiting room. My name was called, and I followed a nurse down a bright hallway into exam room 3. A few moments later Dr. Catano came in and asked what it was I wanted. Having done my research, I pleaded my case, telling him of my lower self-esteem, anxiety, and social fear. I showed him printouts from my parents' health insurance company, which was the hall pass I needed in order to have my blood drawn twice a month, a requirement with this medication. I begged him to help me. For some reason, he agreed to put me on the drug. I was ecstatic.

In my first month on Accutane, my three to four zits turned into eight or ten. By the second month they'd grown to fourteen, then sixteen. My skin became dry, and the acne spread to my back. By the fourth month, I couldn't look at myself in the mirror. I walked around without making eye contact with anyone, avoided friends and parties, and canceled plans. I was becoming concerned that perhaps the risk of depression and self-harm I'd been warned about wasn't so far-fetched. I finally called Dr. Catano. A few days later, when he walked into my exam room and asked how I was doing, I burst into tears. "I thought this would take it away! I thought this would take it away!"

Maybe you can relate to my sense of desperation at unmet expectations. It's like what happens to many of us when we first accept Christ and expect to wake up the next morning without any temptations, addictions, or struggles. As if grace were a magic pill we could swallow and make all the bad stuff disappear. Of course, that's unrealistic. It's also a very narrow view of grace and what it does. It's like trying to take in the vastness of God's grace by looking through a keyhole.

There is a verse from one of my favorite bands, Brand New, where the lead singer opens up about the deep ache of isolation he feels within. He begins to question aloud to Jesus, saying, "What did you do those three days you were dead? Cause this problem's gonna last more than the weekend."[1] Isn't that the truth?

Dr. Catano walked over to where I sat in a small gray chair and put one hand on my shoulder. "It is working," he said in a fatherly voice. "Sometimes it just has to get worse before it gets better. Accutane is forcing all the acne out of your system. You're going to be fine."

Over the next eight weeks, my face cleared up. I felt like an entirely new person. The overwhelming insecurity dissolved, and I regained my confidence. It certainly wasn't the magic bullet I'd hoped for, and the process was much more painful than I'd expected. But having endured it, I did eventually find myself on the other side of the struggle.

The True Essence of Grace

I have thought of the dermatologist's words many times since that day. In countless situations I have had to remind myself that things must sometimes get worse before they get better. And that I will be fine.

At that time it didn't feel true. My situation felt hopeless, shameful, and irreparably broken. During those months of my life I was unable to hide my flaws. There they were, all over my face for everyone to see. I had no control over others' perception of me, and that was painful. Intense shame had driven me to force myself into a regime with a dangerous drug, all to get the results I assumed would make me okay again.

Shame drives a lot of why we do what we do, doesn't it? Over the years as I've wrestled with why people do what they do, I've come to see that most of us carry with us an incomplete understanding of grace.

For me the godfather of grace is Brennan Manning. I'll never forget the time my counselor handed me two of Manning's classics, *Abba's Child* and *The Ragamuffin's Gospel: Good News for the Bedraggled, Beat-Up, and Burnt Out* and asked me to have them read by my next session. I had never encountered the kind of grace he spoke about within those pages. Just two years before Brennan passed, his memoir released with the perfect three words that defined his life, *All Is Grace*.

Manning wrote these words,

> Sin and forgiveness and falling and getting back up and losing the pearl of great price in the couch cushions but then finding it again, and again, and again? Those are the stumbling steps to becoming Real, the only script that's really worth following in this world or the one that's coming. Some may be offended by this ragamuffin memoir, a tale told by quite possibly the repeat of all repeat prodigals. Some might even go so far as to call it ugly. But you see that doesn't matter, because once you are Real you can't be ugly except to people who don't understand . . . that yes, all is grace. It is enough. And it's beautiful.[2]

From the first time I read those words, I've been striving after the kind of Real he described. It is one of the most beautiful concepts I could ever fathom.

Another voice that I have deeply respected over the years is John Wimber. Formerly a producer for the Righteous Brothers, he later became a pastor with a deep desire to seek God's presence. In his biography, *The Way in Is the Way On*, he shared some of the most profound and compelling examples of grace and the way it touched his life.

If all is grace and the way in is the way on, I sensed this stirring that there was so much more to discover about grace. A professor I deeply respected introduced me to John Wesley, an eighteenth-century theologian who gave me greater insight into how deep and wide the concept of grace goes.

In one of his most famous sermons, Wesley outlined three main stages of grace.[3] The first stage refers to what he calls *prevenient grace*, which is what God does to us. Next comes *justifying grace*, which is what God does for us. And lastly, there is *sanctifying grace*, which is what God does in us through the power of God's Holy Spirit.

In my opinion, Wesley's all-encompassing and holistic approach to grace is all too often missing from the conversations churches are having today. The risk here is that we learn to see grace as a get-out-of-jail-free card, something God gives us to use whenever we need a quick fix for the uncomfortable consequences of our choices. If we're not careful, we treat grace like one of those big red buttons in the old Staples commercials. Press here, and *poof!* A clean slate. A fresh start. This is not wrong on its own, but it's also not the full story of grace. The greatness of sanctifying grace is found in God's incredible lifelong commitment to making us whole, holy, and spiritually healthy.

Technology has given us a front-row seat to watch and share our lives through platforms such as social media, podcasts, and blogs. We can feel like we know someone we've never actually met, developing emotional and even spiritual bonds in virtual form. Especially in these online spaces, we also choose the type of truth we want to present, all the while keeping the parts we don't want seen hidden. We can edit those less-than-perfect pieces right out of the picture so that what we post and share looks a lot like authenticity. We can put a filter on it and get the internal boost that comes from being vulnerable without addressing the thing beneath the thing. Instead of becoming whole, holy, and spiritually healthy, we stay the course of living a fractured, pothole-laden, on-the-verge-of-creating-sinkholes-for-all-who-come-in-contact-with-you kind of life. But all the curated messiness that we post without doing the actual work gives us the feeling that we're making progress when in actuality we're not.

This faux vulnerability projects an air of effortlessness, when the truth is it's anything but. Just compare Instagram to an AA meeting. Both are platforms of vulnerability, yet one is filled with filters to make you *look* good, and the other is unfiltered so you can see that you *are* good. Without experiencing the grace that comes with accountability, we miss out on the fullness of God, and we miss out on the growth he longs to develop in us.

I once had the honor of hearing a friend reflect on what his mentor had meant to him. He shared that for years they would speak by phone every morning at 6:50 to discuss their fears and confess their struggles and shame to each other. This man talked with such depth and humility about the transforming work God was doing within him because of these phone calls. After hearing this, I couldn't shake the simple fact that for years this had been going on under the radar. It never made its way on a blog post or Instagram post. It was just as Eugene Peterson would say, "a long obedience in the same direction."[4] No fanfare. No likes or retweets. Just a spiritual exercise between two people committed to trying to embody the fullness of grace. These phone calls were not just confessing but honing in on the triggers that set them off and the long-lost wounds and potholes they hadn't ever addressed but now had the courage to fill with grace.

Confessing our flaws and letting others see our imperfect parts takes a willingness to admit our shortcomings, and it also requires a commitment to change. We can't expect to grow toward healthy spirituality if we refuse to follow up with more than an apology and a promise to do better. It's like saying, "I'm sorry" to get myself off the hook, then turning around and doing the same thing again.

We have a family rule for apologizing in our house. If someone says, "You hurt me," we have to pause and reflect. As we try to practice this with our kids, we find it's much easier to say than do. But we've managed to teach them to say three things.

First, to apologize. "I'm sorry."

Then to check in. "Are you okay?"

And last, to ask forgiveness. "Will you forgive me?"

Sometimes this takes the form of a fairly insincere shout by a sibling, but more often than not it leads to a gentle posture and removes an emotional sting that would otherwise fester.

I'm sorry.

Are you okay?

Will you forgive me?

These questions force the offender to sit with the offended and embrace the ways they've been hurt. They ask for humility, for an embracing of the uncomfortability of bearing witness to the consequences of our actions. They also invite the offended to extend grace and watch as it is accepted, leaving an impact far greater and lasting than a simple, forced "I'm sorry."

Years ago, I sat across at a conference table with my coworkers in a business meeting that had turned into a sort of intervention. I'll never forget having to look into the face of a friend and say, "You are someone I deeply love and respect, but there seems to be a pattern of you sharing the same issues over and over. It feels reminiscent of someone I knew who, for instance, was able to admit they had a substance addiction yet didn't want to do anything about it. I'm worried about you, and I wonder if you notice the patterns I'm seeing. Can you help me understand why this is happening?"

I recall how my friend's eyes welled up as he answered. "I just don't know how to get from here to there. I'm overwhelmed and I feel paralyzed, and I'm really struggling."

By now I, too, had teared up, and I leaned across the table to meet my friend in his key moment of vulnerability. But just then another coworker jumped in to offer the standard Christian response. He said, "Remember the grace you've received! It's washed you clean. You're a good man. Don't get lost in works. Just grab hold of what God gave you through Jesus' death, burial, and resurrection."

The energy and passion of the coworker and the utterance of the word "resurrection" moved the room. Clapping started. "That's right!" someone said. "Amen!"

Just like that, the chance at authentic connection disappeared. My friend had opened up about a messy personal struggle, and instead of making room for it, someone essentially told him to clean it up and be thankful for God's grace. I was furious but confused, unsure of what exactly had just happened.

It wasn't until later, when I was driving home, that I had a chance to process why I'd felt like a wrong had been done. There was a profound disconnect between the grace being proclaimed and the true essence of sanctifying grace—that is, the grace God does *in* us. I'm all for self-awareness and being honest and human about the parts of our stories that fall short of what we desire for our lives, but let's get one thing straight: self-awareness is not spiritual transformation. It's a good first step toward becoming more like Christ, but I'm often surprised by the resistance and pushback to the process of sanctifying grace. Sadly, some believe that working on our inner lives is akin to trying to earn God's grace. They think the notion of heart work and healing is an absurd one. And when you look at it that way, it makes some kind of sense. But my coworker had implied that grace is perfected in us already, and any struggle my friend was sharing had already been fixed by grace. The implication was that my friend did not need to work on healing his wounds but to simply believe that God already had. With a view like that, we miss out on getting to partner with God in our own spiritual growth.

Saying Yes to Grace

Dallas Willard once said, "Grace is not opposed to effort, it's opposed to earning."[5] In ten words, Willard encapsulated everything I wish I'd said in response to my friend's vulnerable confession. How perfectly simple and yet how true. I can never earn my standing or place with Christ; but every day is a choice to practice living into this new reality.

I'll never forget the day my son was born. It was a long delivery and at a few moments a little bit scary. Early in the morning on April 5, Emerson was born, and after a few minutes a nurse turned toward me and said, "Here you go, Dad. Here's your son!" It was the first time I had ever been called "dad," and in that moment I realized that this nurse I had never met before had just given me a title that I'd spend the rest of my life living up to and into! The same thing happened the day I married my wife, when my mentor Rob, who was officiating our wedding, proclaimed that we were now husband and wife. The same thing happened when I said yes to Christ. I was given the titles "son, disciple, beloved." There is nothing I could do to earn these titles, but as Willard writes, it will take effort to fully embody what these titles truly represent.

Dad.

Husband.

Christian.

What we do once we have these new roles is where the heart of this concept meets the pavement. Being called a dad and actually being a dad are two very different things. The same is true for mothers, sons, daughters, spouses, pastors, believers. The same is true for you. You live into these titles by digging in and getting brave and honest with your story.

Grace will find you.

Grace will find you out.

And grace functions to help you become whole, holy, and spiritually healthy.

In the New Testament, there was a religious leader named Saul who was dead set on stopping this movement of grace that was popping up all over the ancient Near East. In Acts 9, Saul found himself on a 150-mile trek to Damascus, having heard stories of people boldly living out the teachings of Jesus. He had received handwritten instruction from religious leaders to put an end to it by whatever (violent) means necessary.

But as Saul was on his way, grace found him. Saul encountered Jesus who said, "Saul, Saul, why do you persecute me?" (v. 4). Saul's eyes were immediately blinded, and he had to be physically led to a man's house in downtown Damascus. For three days, Saul didn't eat or drink anything. Faced with the reality that Jesus was spiritually alive and that the Son of God was who he said he was, Saul must have been haunted by memories of all the harm he'd caused, lives he'd ruined—and taken.

Grace will find you, and grace will find you out.

On the third day of his stay, there was a knock at the door. A disciple named Ananias had come to see Saul. Ananias walked up to the man responsible for the maiming and murdering of his friends. "Brother Saul," he simply said to Christianity's newest convert (v. 17).

Brother. Can you imagine what that word must have meant to Saul given the depths of shame he was in? What a balm. What a grace.

That was the day Saul said yes to grace. But for the next three years, before he ever delivered a sermon or wrote an epistle, he went to work on himself. Following this inner work, he changed his name to Paul, whom we have come to know as the prominent writer of much of our New Testament.

I do wish Paul would have written in one of his letters about what took place during those three years, if only because I'm curious and a fan of history. Regardless, I'm grateful he knew better than to rush to a stage and start preaching. Instead he leaned hard into the work and allowed God to remake his heart, develop his gifts, and prepare him for all that was to come.

Grace has a deep desire to make you whole, holy, healed, and spiritually healthy.

Remember when news reports first began leaking that Tiger Woods had been in an accident? The details continued to expand, and before long we were reading about how, in fact, his wife had chased him down and smashed his car with his golf clubs. We were all privy to a slow drip of salacious information—the accident, the marital fight, then the text messages that revealed an affair. Then we learned he'd been intimate with multiple women. Then we were shocked to hear of his involvement with the porn industry and his sexual addiction. And finally, the truth about his dependency on painkillers and other drugs came to light. Who was this icon, really? We all thought we knew. So cool and collected on the course. Looked up to by so many.

We could hardly believe all that was being said about him. I know I didn't want to believe any of it. At first, I was absolutely floored. Tiger was on top of the world. He seemed untouchable. He had everything he could have ever wanted. Or so it seemed. But "what good is it for someone to gain the whole world, yet forfeit their soul?" (Mark 8:36).

When I was young and new at driving on my own, I thought avoiding a ticket, even when I was clearly speeding, was a show of God's grace. Or if I didn't complete an assignment but my teacher let me off the hook. Hey, another act of grace!

But when you or I don't receive the consequences we deserve, we've been shown mercy, not grace.

Mercy vs. Grace

When my son, Emerson, was almost five, he came running into the kitchen one morning and told my wife and me that he'd had a dream about the baby in Mama's tummy. "I know what the baby's name is going to be," he said matter-of-factly. We braced ourselves. Lately he'd been proudly telling anyone who would listen that the baby was going to be called Dino Slasher. Emerson looked up at us and said, "God wants us to call her Mercy." My wife teared up.

"What does that word mean to you, pal?" I asked.

His response was priceless. "The gift no one deserves."

We melted and agreed at that moment to call our new baby Mercy, which she has been to our family in countless ways since.

If we can define mercy as not getting what we deserve, what do we say of grace?

Maybe grace is allowing your potholes to be fully found out and beginning the beautiful struggle from brokenness to whole, holy, healed, and spiritually healthy. Remember: grace isn't opposed to effort. Grace wants to partner with you in renewing all things pertaining to your heart, soul, and mind.

Whenever you exercise enough courageous curiosity to lean into your greatest sorrows and struggles, you open yourself up to experience the freedom and breakthrough God desires for you. Your potholes won't become sinkholes. You will reach the other side of your break-out. Of your shame. Where things now feel worse, you can trust that they're getting better.

When you're triggered, you remember that your discomfort isn't an obstacle to hide from but a sign there's more work to be done.

Again, the Welcome Prayer speaks to our journey here: "I welcome everything that comes to me today because I know it's for my healing. I welcome all thoughts, feelings, emotions, persons, situations, and conditions."[6]

We can welcome all thoughts, even frightening ones.

All feelings, even negative ones.

All persons, even difficult ones.

And all circumstances, even uncomfortable ones.

Because healing grace is there in the midst, leveraging it all for our spiritual and emotional growth.

I can welcome it all because I understand deep in my bones this might be the very thing that will lead to my healing. Maybe this is one aspect of what Rabbi Paul meant when he said, "Take captive every thought" (2 Cor. 10:5).

Because those most vulnerable thoughts, the ones we're triggered by, the ones that send us into hiding, are the very ones that will take your one and only life where it was designed to go.

So let's not push back or freeze up or slap on a mask. Let's welcome it all as an invitation to get curious. To humble ourselves and discover what grace on grace on grace looks like in your life.

DIG A LITTLE DEEPER

1. Take a moment and get really honest by filling in these blanks:
   When I'm triggered by _____
   _____, I choose (hideouts, insecurities, narratives, grace)
   _____, because
   (what led to this) _____
   and become (what happens inside you and through you) _____
   _____.

   If you had to sum up what you think grace is, how would you answer?

2. Living into the fullness of who God made us to be begs some questions from us:
   • Why do we do what we do?
   • What is our motivation?
   • Is it to earn grace or favor or accolades? Or is it to open ourselves up to be more of who God made us to be?

3. One of the reasons we often push away grace is that we fear it will get worse before it gets better. In what area in your life are you pushing health and wholeness away because it might get worse before it gets better?

08

———

BE STRONG IN GRACE

Guts is grace under pressure.

—ERNEST HEMINGWAY

Grace and peace to you.

—THE APOSTLE PAUL, 1 CORINTHIANS 1:3

AT ASHLEY PARK ELEMENTARY SCHOOL IN CHARLOTTE, North Carolina, there is a fifth-grade teacher named Barry White Jr. who has created a personal handshake for each of his students based on their unique personality. Every day the students line up and before entering the classroom, Mr. White welcomes each student with their very own signature greeting. This combination of claps, snaps, and dance moves lifts the spirits of each student as they feel seen, known, and loved by their teacher.[1]

Of course, our use of handshakes and high fives to greet one another isn't unique to the United States, and it also isn't new. In fact, in the ancient Near East, the standard Hebraic greeting for every interaction was simply "shalom." Although the simplest definition for this word, the one we are most familiar with, is "peace," it actually finds its roots in the word *wholeness*. Shalom encompasses the idea of becoming healthy and whole on the inside and out. Shalom is the aspiration for the world to be put back to right, for order to come to raging chaos. For that profound exhale that happens when you know deep inside that everything is going to be okay.

Don't we long for that moment when we can truly rest easy?

A few years after the death, burial, and resurrection of Jesus, something fascinating happened. The word *grace* was added to the ancient shalom greeting. Christian brothers and sisters began to greet one another by saying, "Grace and peace." These two words came to encompass what the Christian experience was all about. It was like a short breath prayer, serving to connect one another with what Christ had done and what he promised to continue doing. With every interaction, in that time of great potential anxiety, the greeting acted as a fresh reminder to stay present to both the grace and the shalom available to all.

For Paul, these weren't lofty theological concepts or ideals—they were experiential. Confirmation of the truth of the gospel, with deep personal meaning.

When Paul wrote to his mentee, Timothy, he began one of his letters with these words:

> I thank Christ Jesus our Lord, who has given me strength, that he considered me trustworthy, appointing me to his service. Even though I was once a blasphemer and a persecutor and a violent man, I was shown mercy because I acted in ignorance and unbelief. The grace of our Lord was poured out on me abundantly, along with the faith and love that are in Christ Jesus.
>
> Here is a trustworthy saying that deserves full acceptance: Christ Jesus came into the world to save sinners—of whom I am the worst. But for that very reason I was shown mercy so that in me, the worst of sinners, Christ Jesus might display his immense patience as an example for those who would believe in him and receive eternal life. Now to the King eternal, immortal, invisible, the only God, be honor and glory for ever and ever. Amen. (1 Tim. 1:12–17)

Did you catch that? *"Even though* I was once a blasphemer and a persecutor and a violent man, I was shown mercy" (v. 13).

Even though. Such powerful words.

If you were to get really honest, how would you finish this sentence: "Even though I was once a _____ and a _____ and a _____, I was shown mercy"?

I imagine Paul saying the words "grace and peace" multiple times a day, perhaps often with tears in his eyes. The reminder would help him cope with the pain he had brought to many during his season of persecution and violence.

Grace in Super-Beyond-Increasing Abundance

In the next verse, we read, "The grace of our Lord was poured out on me *abundantly*" (v. 14). The word "abundantly" is only used here in the New Testament, and Paul pretty much coined the phrase by adding the prefix "hyper" to the word *abundant*, effectively changing the meaning to "super-beyond-increasing abundance." So this grace Paul referred to, this kind of undeserved favor, is super beyond increasing. It never runs out!

Next, Paul instructed Timothy that he needed to claim these words as his own, just as Paul needed to. That is, that "Christ Jesus came into the world to save sinners" of whom Paul claimed to be the worst (v. 15). Paul was reminding Timothy, "If Christ can do this for me, if grace can do this for me, imagine what he might be able to do for you!"

Paul once more described himself as the worst of sinners because he always carried full knowledge of the pain he had caused. But look what he did to attend to that personal pothole. He clung for dear life to the part of his story in which he was shown mercy. Paul proclaimed the holy purposes of Christ Jesus to leverage Paul's story "as an example for those who would believe in him and receive eternal life" (v. 16).

Whenever Paul said "grace," he was referring to himself as the worst of sinners.

When Paul said grace, he was talking about a super-beyond-increasing abundance of favor and grace.

When Paul said grace, he was referring to Christ coming into the world to save it.

When Paul said grace, he was thinking of what took place on the cross.

Every time Paul said grace, he was remembering the immense patience and forbearance Christ exemplified toward him.

This, all of this, is the grace that transformed him, making him whole, holy, healed, and spiritually healthy. It was this kind of grace that allowed him to exhale. It was only grace that could give him peace from his past, his potholes, and the damage wrought by his sinkholes. When Paul greeted someone with "Grace and peace," he meant so much more than "Hi."

Strength and Courage

In his second letter to Timothy, Paul added a few additional words. "Be strong in the grace" (2:1). At first glance, this might sound like Paul's telling him to cling to grace, to hold on to it tightly. But remember Paul's rabbinical training. Under the tutoring of Gamaliel, a leading authority in the Sanhedrin, Paul was deeply familiar with the Hebrew Scriptures, the traditions, history, and practices of Jewish culture. Paul was riffing on a phrase that had been given to the young leader Joshua many centuries earlier.

But before I unpack this, let's gather some context. Joshua had been Moses' aide for years during the wilderness wandering. One of the first times we read about Joshua is in Exodus 33. "The LORD would speak to Moses face to face, as one speaks to a friend. Then Moses would return to the camp, but his young aide Joshua son of Nun did not leave the tent" (v. 11).

Joshua didn't want to step outside God's presence. It's what he desired, and as an emerging young leader of his time, he was busy developing his character by spending time with God. Often we want to fast-forward past the awkward or hard parts of someone's story and go straight to the highlights reel. But moments of intentionality and diligence are vital to what happens as a result of that work.

After wandering in the desert in northeast Egypt, the people of Israel had slogged through the sand after fleeing Pharaoh and his army. When they finally reached the borders of the promised land, God told Moses to pick one man from each of the twelve tribes of Israel to spy out the land and see how wonderful it was (Num. 13:1–2). One of the men was named Joshua; another was named Caleb. With all twelve men assembled, Moses gave them some instructions. "Go up through the Negev and on into the hill country. See what the land is like and whether the people who live there are strong or weak, few or many. What kind of land do they live in? Is it good or bad? What kind of towns do they live in? Are they unwalled or fortified? How is the soil? Is it fertile or poor? Are there trees in it or not? Do your best to bring back some of the fruit of the land" (vv. 17–20).

The twelve spies went out and had their adventure, and then they returned. All twelve reported that the land was a garden spot. Nobody could deny that. But ten of the twelve were scared. They'd lost the perspective that they were children of the Most High. They'd forgotten the plagues and the parting of the Red Sea. They'd started seeing things from a human perspective, and in fact they didn't perceive themselves to appear very mighty compared to the Amalekites and other groups in the land.

But Caleb remembered the God they served. Still, the ten spies shouted him down.

Then a second man agreed with Caleb's report, Joshua. It was time for him to speak up or sit down. This was his moment. What would Joshua say? Would he take the side of the ten, or would he stand up, own the moment, and inspire his people to do the thing God was inviting them into?

> Joshua son of Nun and Caleb son of Jephunneh . . . tore their clothes and said to the entire Israelite assembly, "The land we passed through and explored is exceedingly good. If the LORD is pleased with us, he will lead us into that land, a land flowing with milk and honey, and will give it to us. Only do not rebel against the LORD. And do not be afraid of the people of the land, because we will devour them. Their protection is gone, but the LORD is with us. Do not be afraid of them."
>
> But the whole assembly talked about stoning them. (Num. 14:6–10)

If you've ever been in this kind of position, you know exactly what Joshua and Caleb were feeling. They had the choice to stay quiet and go with what the group was saying. Or to speak up in faith and step into what they felt God was doing.

Been there?

Here's the beautiful mystery. You and I don't know what might come from these moments of decision. What I've come to discover is that so many people find themselves still living in the past. It takes up so much real estate in their heads and hearts. The choices, the shame, the pain of what happened. Some of us are fixated on tomorrow. On where we will be someday. It's all we think about. We worry and strategize, anxious for what tomorrow will bring. Will we be okay?

Whenever we focus on yesterday or tomorrow, we're missing out on the present moment. This is one of the great tricks of the enemy to pull us from this moment into the events that took place at another time or into the worry of what tomorrow will bring.

The only thing we can truly control is our response to this moment right here and now. If you learn to be attentive to the present, it will prepare you for what God has in store for you, but if not, we risk missing opportunities and end up slowing down our personal, emotional, and spiritual development.

Think about it. When Joshua spent time in God's presence, he had no idea what he was being prepared for. And when he heard the fears of his peers, he must have wondered what they might do. What they might think. How they will respond to him moving forward. But he had a decision to make. Which voice would be loudest in his life? When he stood up to declare what the Hebrew people must do, he had no idea how that one action was preparing him for the next thing God had in mind for him.

You know the rest of the story. The people didn't side with Joshua and Caleb. They preferred to side with the doubters, and God condemned them to forty years of wandering in the wilderness until that entire generation of naysayers died. They did a U-turn and headed back into the wasteland. There would still be miracles, and God would be present with them day and night. Yet it was a time of disappointment, defeat, and punishment.

Fast-forward through the books of Numbers and Deuteronomy. At the end of Deuteronomy, when the years of wandering were over, Moses died. He'd been leading the people for all those years. And he died at the edge of the promise.

A vacuum of leadership followed. But God knew Joshua was ready to take on Moses' mantle. So he spoke to him (Josh. 1:1–11).

And look at what God said. "As I was with Moses, so I will be with you; I will never leave you nor forsake you. Be strong and courageous" (vv. 5–6).

Strength and courage.

Three times in four verses, God said, "Be strong and courageous."

In Hebrew, this phrase is *Rak Chazak* and it became a battle cry for future generations of the Hebrews. Similar to William Wallace in *Braveheart* screaming, "They may take our lives, but they'll never take our freedom!"[2]

Imagine the scene. Warriors suiting up for battle, psyching themselves up for conflict. They start chanting. "Rak Chazak! Rak Chazak!" They line up for battle, and when the commander gives the order, they run to glory.

Getting ready for battle is one time you might utter "Rak Chazak." But you might also say it when you're unsure of yourself. This can be a prayer of desperation. "Lord, I need your help. Please make me strong and courageous!" The phrase became my anthem during one of the hardest seasons of my life. I'd wake up early in the morning and walk a neighboring trail. If I'm honest I didn't think I had what it takes to meet the demands of my reality. This simple battle cry was something I could shout or whisper, something that helped me call on greater spiritual and emotional courage than I could produce on my own.

Always Enough Grace

I imagine Joshua wondered if he had what it would take. Wasn't the job of being Moses' successor too big a role for him? I believe God knew his fears and insecurities and was saying, "Be strong and courageous, my son. Don't be afraid. As I was with Moses, I'll be with you. I'll never leave you nor forsake you. Rak Chazak, Joshua."

Now Joshua had a choice. Would he step up or step aside?

"All right," he said, in effect "I'll try. I'm not Moses. I'm Joshua. But I'm going to take you at your word, God. This is my moment. I will lead the Hebrew people into the promised land."

Jump forward to Paul writing his final letter to his mentee, Timothy. Kicking off chapter 2 with, "Be strong in the grace that is in Christ Jesus." It's like Paul knew that young leaders were faced with the choice to run away from their triggers and challenges or to hold fast and embrace them as opportunities to grow. Paul wanted Timothy to have that Rak Chazak strength, but for it to be in grace. To be so confident in the super-beyond-increasing abundance of grace, which never runs out. Paul gave Timothy a battle cry, a fresh reminder, a powerful word to claim in his moment. To Rak Chazak in grace and watch how God would guide and lead him.

If you are at all like me, you know too well what it feels like when we miss our moments. In conversations with my wife when something is said, I can get triggered and choose to be strong in defensiveness, which never helps me, my relationship with my wife, or my journey to wholeness. I can be strong in my own selfishness, where I think about my needs above others. I can be strong in escape and do whatever it takes to not address the pothole that is quickly becoming a sinkhole. Or sometimes it's just that I'm strong in distraction and my mind is somewhere else, and I miss what God has put right before me. Instead of grace and peace, I find myself more filled with regret and pain.

To be strong in grace is to grow profoundly curious about the thing beneath the thing.

To become more comfortable being uncomfortable, acknowledge places in your story where you have been the worst of sinners.

To discover that "even though" you were once _____ and _____ and _____, Christ poured out his abundant grace on you and showcased his immense patience.

To be strong in grace means to be patient with your process of getting after the thing beneath the thing. Some of these wounds take more time to heal than others. Some of your potholes may require professional help for the sake of being fully healed. But through our curiosity, our patience, and tenacity, and by digging ever deeper into our story, we can find the freedom that comes with knowing true grace. Grace never runs out. There's always more than enough to go around.

Of course, grace also makes room for those times we will fall into old habits, old patterns, and old ways of dealing with our pain. Setbacks aren't failures as much as a clue that you need to dig deeper. When I would share my setbacks with those closest in my life, I realized how much instant shame would hover over me. It was like I had forgotten everything about grace and started believing that my shame was greater. I'll never forget sharing one time with my friend about a particularly painful wound in my story. He expressed that he could see and feel the shame connected to my setback. Then he simply said, "Be kind to yourself, Steve, and try being more kind to your story."

Learning to be kind to yourself in the face of a setback is crucial if you want to discover and glean more about the why behind your decision. At the moment it can be hard to allow yourself what may feel like an unearned or unfair kindness, but remember that grace is not about what is fair. Remember that it is grace, not shame, that gets to have the final word in your life.

Years ago, during a counseling session, my counselor taught me that when I find myself getting worked up, or afraid, or defensive, to plant my right foot in the conversation and slide my left foot to the side, almost as if the left foot was outside the conversation. Then to shift my weight onto my left foot and start observing. To observe my body, my tone, my words, and my spirit. To ask myself questions like, "Where are you?" and "What's really going on?" and "What is it you desire to come out of this?" or "What is it about this moment that is so frustrating?" and "Why do you think you're getting so worked up?"

They're all simple but effective questions. I've learned I can showcase curiosity and humility in the moment, giving myself the best chance for healing and wholeness. It's when I'm strong in grace that I can extend it to myself, to the plethora of potholes in my story, and to the person who has unfortunately gotten too close to this old wound.

But why is it so hard in the moment? Recently I saw my wife coming toward me, and I could tell she wanted to talk about something, so I slowly got up and moved to the next room. She followed and gently asked, "Can I share something that I've been noticing over the past week?" As I nodded my head, I could feel this inner defense lawyer preparing for my closing argument. Sarah shared how she felt I was more scattered than usual and less present at home with her and our kids. It was at this moment the defense lawyer started to speak internally, *Does she not understand all you do for this family? Nobody sees you. Nobody understands the weight and pressure. You don't deserve this!*

It was here I had a choice. Humility or pride.

Curiosity or anger.

Over the last year I've recognized this pattern again and again that battles within me. One of the most helpful tools I've learned comes from the great Dallas Willard around what he called the vision, intention, and method of Christian formation.[3] Dallas described how one must be ravished with a vision for what their life can truly be in Christ. Think of that moment in John 10:10 when Jesus declared, "I have come that they may have life, and have it to the full."

Once, while my friend TJ and I were talking on the phone, we got to discussing the nuances of John 10:10. I took copious notes, and this line stood out to me: "When you anchor your life in Jesus, you have nothing to prove, nothing to lose, and nothing to hide." That's a vision I can get swept up in. That's the kind of life I want.

Nothing to prove.

Nothing to lose.

Nothing to hide.

But I just can't stop at the vision. Willard would teach that you must have a robust intention that decides to live that kind of life no matter what. It's here that I began to realize why it can be hard when my wife offers up some thoughts on how present I've been at home. It's here I can act out of what Willard referred to as an "impulsive will," where I do what I want to do and say whatever I want to say.

Or I can choose something that will lead to me becoming more formed in the likeness of Christ. Willard refers to this as the "reflective will," where I reflect and ponder if this decision will allow me to truly live out my vision of a life that has nothing to prove, nothing to lose, and nothing to hide.

But here's where it gets to the next level for me. Willard said that our choices over time have this muscle memory connected to them. This is why when we're stressed we often are driven not by vision but by our impulsive will to escape. He called this the "embodied will." This muscle memory is why habits and addictions and generational brokenness are often so hard to break. On the flip side, the muscle memory, also known as embodied will, can grow when we choose to align ourselves with a grander vision. When we're humble. When we can receive feedback without getting defensive. When we love unconditionally, extend grace freely, and choose patience again and again, this healthy embodied will has the power to shape us into that John 10:10 life Jesus desires for us.[4]

The more I become aware of my potholes and masks, the more I realize how I need spiritual exercises or methods that will form me more into Christlikeness. This is what Willard referred to as "means." These are those sacred practices that prepare us when our potholes get triggered to choose to be strong in grace.

So I looked at my wife, recognizing this as a chance to grow closer and get more curious or push her away and be more hardhearted. Or better said, I asked myself, *What will I choose to be strong in?*

Grace or pride?

Trying to win or nothing to prove?

Protecting myself or nothing to lose?

Pushing her away or nothing to hide?

I fought through my own fear and pride and simply said, "Tell me more." And she did, in grace-filled and truthful fashion, allowing me to see what she saw. It led to an honest and human conversation that was deeply connected to potholes formed years and years ago.

With the Rak Chazak battle cry, I can run toward the pain instead of away from it. With this kind of courage, that simple breath prayer of grace and peace becomes accessible and incarnated in my life. I do have the ability to let go of the false scaffolding I've been relying on while constructing a version of myself that can't coexist with the version God envisions for me. One of the most helpful practices to help me embody what it truly means to be strong in grace has been returning again and again to the prayer of welcome I shared earlier and becoming more in tune with what I'm still clutching hold of that's not named grace.

The second part of the Welcome Prayer describes the power of letting go. Let's try personalizing it.

Today, I release my craving for power and control.

I open my hands and let go of my driving desires to be loved and esteemed, approved of by others, and comforted by empty idols.

I release my default survival instincts.

I don't carry the weight of changing any situation, any others around me, or even myself.[5]

Repeating the method of the Welcome Prayer day after day, connected to a clear vision of a life anchored in Jesus as one that has nothing to prove, nothing to lose, and nothing to hide has helped me grow closer to Jesus and begin creating a healthy, more Jesus-focused embodied will rather than an unhealthy Steve-focused embodied will.

DIG A LITTLE DEEPER

1. What do you need to let go of today so you can step into more grace and peace?

2. What are you grasping hold of that seems to be creating more potholes and collateral damage rather than peace and wholeness?

3. What could it look like if you were to replace what you've been clinging to with the immense patience that comes from the super-beyond-increasing abundance called grace?

4. Do you ever struggle with adding another word instead of grace to the end of "be strong in" like I do? These words often are oriented around control, fear, failure, losing, or shame, and come out in defensiveness, frustration, anger, powering up, trying to escape, and hiding.

5. What could your life look like if it were truly anchored in Jesus and you had nothing to prove, nothing to lose, and nothing to hide?

09

IT'S YOUR CHOICE

Some things cost more than you realize.

—RADIOHEAD

*Few people arise in the morning as hungry for God
as they are for cornflakes or toast and eggs.*

—DALLAS WILLARD, *HEARING GOD*

THE APOSTLE PAUL'S MINISTRY SPANNED MORE THAN thirty years and two continents. He was one of God's primary agents in the spread of Christianity from the tiny Roman province of Palestine to the heart of the Roman Empire and, eventually, around the globe. He wrote nearly half the books of the New Testament—thirteen out of twenty-seven—and contributed the second-highest number of words, behind only Luke.

I've studied the words of 2 Timothy 2:3–7, which Paul wrote to Timothy, most of my life, but they have always puzzled me. Let's read them together and I'll explain.

> Join with me in suffering, like a good soldier of Christ Jesus. No one serving as a soldier gets entangled in civilian affairs, but rather tries to please his commanding officer. Similarly, anyone who competes as an athlete does not receive the victor's crown except by competing according to the rules. The hardworking farmer should be the first to receive a share of the crops. Reflect on what I am saying, for the Lord will give you insight into all this.

Why did Paul feel the need to add that Timothy should reflect on all he was saying? It all seemed pretty straightforward. Soldiers, athletes, farmers. Got it. What additional insights were there to be gained? What was so mystical about soldiers, athletes, and farmers, which for Timothy, living in first-century Ephesus, was an everyday sight? Paul didn't always spell things out for Timothy, his beloved young mentee. In verse 7 of the above passage, Paul basically said, "Timothy, my boy, I'm not going to unpack this metaphor for you. Just reflect on my words, and God will explain it."

It puzzled me so much that I decided to do what Paul had suggested Timothy would do. I reflected on the passage and asked God to explain it to me.

Paul described to Timothy (and to us) three characters and three fields. And I've come to believe that an understanding of these characters and fields will help you and me live the most satisfied life possible.

Soldier, athlete, farmer.

Battlefield, athletic field, agricultural field.

To glean a better understanding of the significance of each of these images as Timothy would have understood it, let's visit the ancient Near East and consider Greek and Roman culture.

The Soldier

Our first character is the soldier. Take another look at that part of our passage.

> Join with me in suffering, like a good soldier of Christ Jesus. No one
> serving as a soldier gets entangled in civilian affairs, but rather tries
> to please his commanding officer. (vv. 3–4)

To the Romans, soldiers were important. They had status in society. Children aspired to become soldiers of the Roman army. The empire had been forged by the Legions (soldiers), after all, and the empire was maintained by the Legions. Every good Roman child lived to be a soldier.

Four things were required of any Roman soldier. First, you had to be willing to sacrifice. You had to be ready to give your life for Rome. Makes sense for a soldier, right?

Second, soldiers had to be obedient. *Obedience* is a fascinating, twofold word. To obey, one must listen well. But hearing isn't obeying unless it's paired with instant response. Do you recall a time when you heard the promptings of God but didn't respond quickly? To be obedient to the Lord is to listen, yes, but it's also to move in response to what we hear.

No Roman soldier would ever dare ask his commanding officer why they were given an order. If the commanding officer said to go to battle, it was done. Soldiers placed their trust in and respected their commanding officer. They believed the commanding officer knew best.

Do we ever look up at God and ask, "Why?"

Obedience is hearing plus doing. We have a God who is always whispering, prompting, guiding, leading, and speaking to us. And yet we often find ourselves acting like three-year-olds, not moving, not responding, just sitting there asking, "Why?" When we give to God the same trust a Roman soldier gave his commanding officer, we jump to fulfill his promptings.

In addition to being willing to sacrifice and obey, they had to be loyal. Loyal to Rome. Loyal to their unit. Loyal to their people. Loyal to their commanding officer.

And finally, Roman soldiers had to be devoted to duty. A Roman code forbade any soldier engaged in military occupation from becoming engaged in civilian affairs. Rome didn't want any of its soldiers having multiple commanding officers. They did not want soldiers becoming distracted or conflicted. When the call came to march to battle, the army couldn't wait for thousands of its soldiers to ask for time off from work or an excuse from class. If you were a soldier, that's all you were.

The late Dallas Willard spoke at my alma mater a number of years ago. One of my friends, JJ, got up and interviewed him after his talk. For thirty-plus years, Dallas had been a philosophy teacher at USC, and while he was there he taught the same few classes year in and year out. My friend asked him what he found to be the biggest difference between the incoming freshman class in his first year at USC and the last incoming class he taught, thirty years later.

"That's easy," Dallas said. "All these students now are distracted. Their minds are in a thousand different places. And because of that, they miss out on the kingdom of God breaking in all around them. They miss out on the whispers and the promptings of God."

Perhaps this was why Rome demanded each soldier have only one commanding officer. They must not get distracted. Because if they get distracted, their loyalty, their devotion, their obedience, their sacrifice—all the things that made Rome mighty—might just waver.

As I reflected on these verses, God showed me why Paul instructed Timothy to be a good soldier of Christ Jesus. He was saying that you can have only one commanding officer. You can't be distracted, and you can't be torn in allegiance. You've got to spend your day bringing honor to your commander by following his instructions.

Do you find yourself distracted? Does God see you as devoted to your duty? Or are you being pulled away from the present moment and not fully available to him? Every time we're distracted, we miss out on what God has for us.

Commit to serve your one and only commanding officer with a willingness to sacrifice, with both the hearing and the doing of obedience, with loyalty, and with a singularity of devotion so that when the call comes to march to the battlefield, you are ready to be on the front lines with him.

The Athlete

The second character referenced in this passage is the athlete, and the second field is the athletic field.

> Similarly, anyone who competes as an athlete does not receive the victor's crown except by competing according to the rules. (v. 5)

The athlete and the athletic field were big deals in Roman culture. The Greeks had created the Olympics, and the Romans continued holding the games until 394 CE. The Romans loved athletic competitions. They were all about chasing the crown or the medal. Constantly pushing themselves to win.

In this passage, the idea of an athlete competing according to the rules is encompassed in the Greek phrase *athlein nomimos*. This phrase was crucial in understanding the difference between an amateur and a professional athlete.

I love sports. I played college basketball. Perhaps *play* isn't the right word. I mostly sat on the bench. But I did get free shoes! I still love going to the gym and shooting hoops for fun. The place is often crammed with amateur athletes, very much like me. Sure, we try to look like the pro athletes, from wearing expensive kicks to owning the latest gear. But no matter how good we look, the truth is revealed when the playing begins. That's when we see the difference between rec-league guys and professional athletes.

I'm honored to have friends who have actually competed profes-
sionally. And there is a massive difference, let me tell you, between
us weekend jocks and the real deal. Professional athletes are über-
disciplined with their schedule, in the weight room, in the film room,
with what they put in their bodies, by creating space to get enough
reps in. All so they can keep practicing their craft to the best of their
abilities.

When trying something new for the first time, we all start out
as amateurs. It's a great way to put ourselves out there and discover
what truly interests us, what brings us joy and life and satisfaction. But
most of us keep our hobbies just that, hobbies. We aren't in it to win
it; we don't harbor plans to go pro. We do it for the fun of it, and that's
wonderful. Hobbies can be vital outlets for our mental, emotional, and
spiritual well-being. But sometimes we tap into something that grows
into a professional pursuit.

My wife had this happen with her painting. She'd been into art
since she was a kid, always sketching and drawing. Then in high
school she took a few art classes, which unleashed a passion she hadn't
embraced before. Before long, she was following her dream to become
a professional artist. She opened a gallery, taught art classes, and now
sells her work all over the country. But she didn't start out there. She
had to develop her skills and learn about the process.

I'm sure if I had the chance to sit with you, you could share similar stories about you or someone you know who enjoyed this kind of
experience. At the very least, we all understand that in order to hone a
craft, we've got to commit to getting better at it. We have to put in the
work to get to the next level.

No matter what the field, there's a big difference between the hob-
byist and the professional. Author Malcolm Gladwell says it takes ten
thousand hours of practice to master a skill.[1]

All of this has got me wondering, Where are you in the process of developing your faith? How serious are you about living the life Jesus made available to you?

How many of us, I wonder, are rec-league Christians? Sure, we've got our leather-bound Bibles, our Tomlin and Hillsong and Maverick City albums. We can speak Christianese and pray the right way. But looking the part isn't the same thing as living it.

Your joy and contentment in Christ will rise at the same rate as your seriousness about following him.

When Paul told Timothy he would win the prize only if he played according to the rules, I think he was saying, "Hey, my dear *talmidim*, or disciple, I want you to be a disciple 24/7. I want you to be someone who is hungry, who takes seriously how he views himself and his gifts and his life. Don't be someone who shows up only once in a while. Be someone who is present to the blessing and to the power and to the Spirit of God that is before you. Go pro!"

By the way, all pro athletes know the rules of their sport. They're given a rulebook. If they're in a team sport, they're also given a playbook specific to their team. Some of my friends in the NFL tell me they receive a binder with 650-plus plays listed. And they carry that binder everywhere they go. Why? Because they are expected to know it. To memorize it. And if they don't know the plays within a few weeks, they will be out of a job.

Why do they commit to such a burden? Because they want to win that victor's crown. They want to return to the city they represent and have the entire place yell, "Hail to the victors! Hail to the conquering heroes. Hail to the people who have done it." That's what they long for.

As Christians, we long for the love of Jesus to be known by all. That's why we must take our faith seriously.

How well do you know God's playbook?

The Farmer

Paul's third character is the farmer and the third field is an agricultural field that is filled with crops, as in amber waves of grain.

> The hardworking farmer should be the first to receive a share of the crops. (v. 6)

Farmers played a crucial role in the ancient Near East. If the farms failed, everyone died.

It's probably an understatement to say the farmers were hardworking. Especially back then. They didn't exactly have shiny new John Deere tractors. They were out there with shovels and picks and hoes and oxen. Everything they did, they did by hand, including preparing the ground for seeding.

Have you ever met a farmer? Ever shaken a farmer's hand? My friend Kenneth has a farm in Wyoming, and whenever he attempts to shake my hand, I just give him a fist bump. I've learned the hard way. He'll crush my hand!

Before the sun comes up, they're up and out. And when the sun goes down, they're just beginning to put their tools away. These are hardworking men and women. Their whole job, before a field can be seeded, is to get that soil ready. They've got to till the land and get the weeds out. Only then can they begin to plant and scatter the seeds. Then they've got to water. And they've got to protect the crop because there's dust and bugs and things that are going to want to ruin the fruit.

Know what they do when they've finished all that crushing work? They wait. They pray for the right amount and the perfect timing of rain and sun. Farmers understand patience. They understand hard work, yes, but more than most of us, they know how to wait well.

Our culture doesn't wait well. We want our food faster. We want our internet faster. We want faster delivery. Amazon now has same-day delivery. In some cases, you can get your stuff delivered to your door within an hour. An hour! I'm old enough to remember when you had to allow six weeks for a shipment.

I'm not saying fast is bad, and I'm not knocking anyone's desire for speed. There are many instances in life where speed is a blessing. But here's the problem it presents for us. Sometimes we see the beauty of lightning-fast delivery and the beauty of fast food and the beauty of being handed a cup of great coffee right away, and we think the same should be true with our spiritual formation. Wait a lifetime to be slowly sanctified by the gentle working of the Spirit? No, thank you! I'll have it now, please.

But guess what, my friend. We cannot microwave spiritual formation.

It takes time. It's a process. Like a farmer, you've got to work that soil. You've got to work that land. You've got to protect it and water it. And you've got to wait.

But the payoff is great. After all that waiting you get to experience the harvest. When that harvest comes and you get to pick it and enjoy it, you celebrate. In the ancient Near East, festivals abounded as they harvested the fruit from the vine. The waiting was over, and all their hard work and patience had paid off.

Who Is My Commanding Officer?

As I studied this passage in 2 Timothy, I extracted from it Paul's lessons about being a devoted soldier, a pro athlete, and a patient farmer. Those were fantastic. Those will preach! Yet I still had the sense there was something more there, so I kept meditating on it all and asking for wisdom.

My main question was what these three characters and fields had to do with one another. I mean, they were all great lessons and models on their own, but why had Paul shoved them together into the same paragraph, as if making one point with three illustrations?

"Reflect on what I am saying," Paul wrote, "for the Lord will give you insight into all this" (v. 7).

I racked my brain. What was the "all this"? What does reflecting on being a soldier, an athlete, and a farmer mean to us today? Paul dropped all this insight and knowledge on Timothy and then ran for the door with just a "Hey, son, you figure it out. Don't call me."

For weeks, I dug and meditated and contemplated. I got up at 5:00 a.m. every day and hiked around the desert near our home. *Lord, what do you want me to learn from these stories?*

Slowly some key ideas began to emerge as to what I think Paul hoped to instill in Timothy. The first concerned the idea of a commanding officer. I didn't know what God was saying to me about it yet, only that he wanted me to highlight that word in my mind. *Commander.*

Studying the part about the athlete, I felt God saying to highlight the word *playbook* in my mind. So I did.

Commanding officer. Playbook. What did they have to do with each other? I kept walking and praying and ruminating.

From the story of the farmer, I finally heard God impress upon me the word *harvest.*

I was like, *Commanding officer plus playbook plus harvest? God, I'm reflecting on these ideas like you said. So, what is it you want to show me?*

Into my mind popped a statistic I'd recently come across. Sociologists say we have, every day, an average of thirty-five thousand decisions to make. Every one of us, every day, makes thirty-five thousand choices.[2]

Okay, so now we've got commander plus playbook plus harvest plus tons of choices. *Still not getting it, Lord.*

But the idea of choosing brought to my mind what God told the Hebrew people when they were about to move into the promised land. Deuteronomy 30:19 reads, "This day I call the heavens and the earth as witnesses against you that I have set before you life and death, blessings and curses. Now choose life, so that you and your children may live."

Jews in that time may have been faced with 34,999 other choices to make on that day, but I imagine this one topped the charts.

The Hebrew word underlying "choose" here is *bahar*, which means that the thing you select is the thing you are boldly proclaiming as the best possible way to live. To the Hebrew people, every choice mattered.

Choices matter for us, as well. And every day you have thirty-five thousand of them.

I was on a dusty desert trail on about day nine of that particular thought journey when I sensed God explaining to me, *Hey, here's what I want you to see. While you're making those thirty-five thousand choices every day, who is your commanding officer? Is it me? Or is it somebody else?*

This stopped me in my tracks. I yanked out my pen and a notecard, and I began to write down all of my commanding officers.

Myself

God

The overpowering, suffocating shame that follows me around

Fear

Security, which is often financial

My boss

Then I added an asterisk representing three hurtful comments spoken over me a long time ago that somehow I'd not been able to let go of.

I sensed God prompting me to honestly rank those commanders. *Why? I don't want to!* I knew the "right" ranking would place God at the top of my list, and I knew I wasn't there yet. If I'd said, "Oh, yeah, God, you're number one, and all the others are way down on the list," he'd have recognized my full-on lie.

So I told God I'd spend the next week doing an internal audit to see which ones came to the front and which ones receded.

And here's the order I eventually was forced to assign to my list of commanders.

Myself.
Shame (a close second).
God.
Security.
Fear.
Boss.
Those three lies I'd been told.

I'm guessing you already see the problem here. Not merely that God wasn't first on my list but that I needed a list at all. A soldier isn't allowed to become entangled in civilian affairs. A soldier doesn't have more than one commander. And here I was with seven.

I also noticed that each one of my commanding officers had a different playbook. You don't obey your fears the same way you obey a boss, and what shame asks of you is a lot different from what a quest for security asks of you. Each one carries a different philosophy, a different trajectory, and a different way of directing me to orient my life.

Also, each commander and each playbook produces a different

kind of harvest. For example, when I play according to the playbook of those lies spoken over me, I'll harvest defeat, victimhood, and rage.

No wonder we end up in such painful places in our life journeys, when we are allowing ourselves to be manipulated by false gods and false narratives.

It's not hard to find places where the commanding officer + playbook + harvest dynamic plays out. It's all around us, in the news, on Twitter, in conversations with friends and family. Some people are completely and profoundly driven by money. Money is their commanding officer. It's why they get up in the morning. More money. More money. More money. More money. Their playbook is typically the *Wall Street Journal*, *Forbes*, or perhaps some business leader whose footsteps they work to follow. At the end of their life, what will this person reap?

They might have harvested some money, but it's usually never enough to satisfy. It's certainly stressful to manage and guard. And underneath it all, what they've often harvested is greed.

Recently, on a plane, I was flipping through the American Airlines in-flight magazine. When I got to the end, I spotted an ad for a protein bar with a picture of a seventyish-year-old man. Shirtless and bald, but he was ripped. The ad seemed to whisper, "This could be you," and I wasn't quite sure how to feel about that.

Ads selling us a better life are impossible to avoid. You can't buy groceries without seeing them lining the checkout kiosk, and unless you're paying for premium, they are blasting into your homes every day via Spotify and Hulu. What are they selling? Image. Lifestyle. And if that's your commanding officer—how you look, how you feel about your body—if that's everything that matters, what's your playbook going to be?

At the end of my life, there probably won't be a group of people going, "Hey Steve, can you take off your shirt one more time? We just really wanna see your muscles." At least, I hope not. In all seriousness, that's the last thing *anyone* is going to be thinking about. All this body image stuff is not transferable to the next reality. A great physical image is a pitiful harvest in light of eternity. And even in this life probably all it will seed is narcissism.

What if shame is your commanding officer? The shame storms are always close, ready to bring thunder, lightning, and a downpour of past things that you've said or done. They want to grab all your energy and all your focus and shift it to the past.

For many of us, this is our story. Shame is our commander, so we adopt shame's playbook. We're constantly mindful of the things we have done wrong and the ways we have hurt other people and ourselves. We remember the neglect or abandonment. We remember the hurtful things we've spoken and the lies we've told. All of that shame follows us.

What will be the harvest of playing by the rules of shame and obeying shame as our commanding officer? Self-pity. Self-loathing. All of it leading to a downward spiral of contempt and a cesspool of despair.

Your commanding officer determines your playbook, which determines your harvest.

Battlefield, athletic field, agricultural field.

I think that's what Paul wanted Timothy to think about in his letter. It's definitely what I got out of it.

The good news is that once you know what's going on here, you can choose your commander. Identify who you're following, and then, if you don't like what you find, make a command change. You're the president, so you can fire your chairman of the joint chiefs if you don't like where they're taking the country.

Are you living with rival commanding officers? Are you happy with their orders and their playbook and your harvest?

If not, have a little insurrection and overthrow the boss. There needs to be, once and for all, a regime change. You must come to the moment when you declare that no rogue commander—shame, fear, anger, money, image, even yourself—will be your commander. None of them will ever again be the primary voice in your head.

Who did Paul say should be our commanding officer? He instructed Timothy to be "a good soldier of Christ Jesus" (2 Tim. 2:3).

Can you imagine what your life would be like if Jesus really were your commanding officer? How would your life be different? What orders would he send down? What playbook would he use? What would the harvest of your life be?

I don't know about you, but to me that sounds a lot better than multiple commanders giving conflicting orders that all lead to a harvest other than God's intention.

Commander Jesus is our model. He was the perfect soldier himself, always obeying his Father's orders, which is what makes him our perfect commander. He meets all four criteria. He sacrificed for us. He was obedient to the Father. He was loyal to the kingdom. And he was so devoted to you and me that he gave himself up so we could fully live.

So many Christians, myself included, have to ask ourselves an embarrassingly high number of times if we really do trust that the Lord knows best. But lock that one down. Nail it down once and for all that Jesus is a trustworthy, reliable commander who has your best in mind.

Once you trust in Jesus as your commander, the question becomes, What is your playbook?

Which Playbook Do I Choose?

If you've decided to follow Jesus as commander, your playbook is the Bible.

Paul reminded his dear student, Timothy, that "all Scripture is

God-breathed and is useful for teaching, rebuking, correcting and training in righteousness" (2 Tim. 3:16).

The Bible, our playbook, is God-breathed. Which means every word in it matters. Every word can and will be used as God's vocabulary to us today. It's not some outdated concept that lost its relevance millennia ago. The crazy thing about this Book is that these words still inspire and propel us today.

Second, all Scripture is useful for teaching. It's the playbook that will teach you how to live, how to enjoy a satisfied life.

Third, the Bible is useful for rebuking. None of us likes to be rebuked. As the writer of Hebrews said, "No discipline seems pleasant at the time, but painful. Later on, however, it produces a harvest of righteousness and peace for those who have been trained by it" (Heb. 12:11). I mean, we might later come to appreciate and even be grateful for it, but it's never pleasant in the moment. But rebuking is lifesaving. A good, kind Father wants to make sure you stay on track, and he is there to gently guide you when you do inevitably go off course.

One way Scripture tends to rebuke me is when I begin to listen to multiple commanding officers. That is a good, kind rebuke, but it isn't pleasant in the moment.

God's Word doesn't just teach us and it doesn't just rebuke us—it also corrects us. If our ears are tuned to God's Spirit, He'll use the Word to show us as soon as we get even half a degree off course. The Scriptures will correct us, straighten our path, and allow us to stay focused on the only commanding officer worthy of our allegiance.

The final thing Paul reminded Timothy regarding God's Word is that it's useful for "training in righteousness." God's playbook will train you to be the kind of disciple who understands the most beautiful way to live.

To the Hebrew people, righteousness could never be separated from the ideas of justice and shalom. Remember that shalom is like peace, plus much more. It is wholeness and freedom, God's perfect intention for mankind. Every time we are trained in righteousness, we come near to justice and to God's dream for how the world will be. And when we live righteously, with Jesus as our commanding officer, we bring justice to this world. We bring this world closer to what God intended it to be.

That's what Scripture helps us do. It trains us. Corrects us. Rebukes us. Teaches us. For what purpose? "So that the servant of God may be thoroughly equipped for every good work" (2 Tim. 3:17).

In other words, it helps you and me get to the thing beneath the thing, so that we can move to the other side of pain. So we can live our most whole, holy, and spiritually healthy life.

What Do I Hope to Harvest?

The commander and playbook you choose determine your harvest. What do you want your harvest to be? In other words, what do you desire the outcome of your life to be?

To have a clearer vision of a specific outcome it sometimes helps to verbalize it. For instance, no one wants a life of bitterness; we just don't realize that playing by the bitterness playbook will bring about that result. Jealousy is a poor commander, but it will certainly produce the same predictable outcome. Similarly, obeying love and kindness, and living out those playbooks—chiefly, the Bible—will result in a kind and loving harvest. The outcome, the harvest, is determined by what we obey and by whose playbook we follow.

If you want the harvest that comes from a life of following Christ, you've got to overthrow all other commanders and install Jesus on the throne. Pick your ending, then decide which commander to follow. Ask the Spirit to help you capture every thought and tune out everyone else's commands.

When you understand that God is a good, kind Father, that Jesus came in grace and truth, and that it's in God's character to rebuke and to correct, but also to teach and to train you for your good—it's overwhelming!

When you're grounded in knowing that he loves and accepts you no matter what, the Bible becomes a playbook that shows you exactly how to harvest the best things. You'll harvest the satisfied life, yes. But in God's economy true satisfaction comes from harvesting the thing that the Father most cares about, the only thing that you can take into the next reality.

People.

When Jesus is your commanding officer, every decision you make in line with his commands and his playbook will lead you to see people as God sees them. And to love them the way he does.

DIG A LITTLE DEEPER

1. What or who are your commanding officers? Why not take a minute to jot down a list that you can reflect on this week? To be difference makers, we need to be sure we're following the right commander.
2. Who or what is the loudest voice in your life?
3. What is your go-to playbook?
4. What have you been trying to harvest in your life?
5. What do you want others to say about you at your funeral? What harvest do you want to reap today and at the end of your life?

10

———

THE POWER OF CONNECTION

We belong to each other.

—MOTHER TERESA

If you remain in me and I in you,
you will bear much fruit.

—JESUS, JOHN 15:5

A FEW YEARS BACK I HAD THE PRIVILEGE TO TRAVEL OVER-seas and meet with a global partner serving in South Africa. A few of us who were traveling together planned to stay on-site at an academy. But due to a scheduling conflict, there were no beds available. The director felt terrible and told us he had secured two options. One, a hotel in town. The other, a little bungalow on a neighboring vineyard. A few of my friends snagged the hotel option. But I knew my answer as soon as I heard the word *vineyard*.

After settling in, I began each morning by reading John 15, and I adopted three essential practices to help keep me focused.

Let's start with the importance of the vine.

The vine was the nationalistic symbol to the Hebrew people. Isaiah, David, Ezekiel, Jeremiah, and Hosea all wrote about this. At the very top of King Herod's temple were golden clusters of grapes on a vine, which stood six feet tall. The vine symbolized God's favor and blessing.

When he declared, "I am the true vine, and my Father is the gardener," Jesus was saying he was the fulfillment of all the hopes and desires of his people (John 15:1).

And when he added that his Father was the gardener, he meant Father God was the one with the shears. The one with the grander vision for the vine. The one who does the pruning.

Jesus went on to say, "[The gardener] cuts off every branch in me that bears no fruit, while every branch that does bear fruit he prunes so that it will be even more fruitful" (v. 2). One of the key roles of a vinedresser is to prune growth as the plants expand.

Trust the Pruning

The first essential practice in order to hone your skills is to *trust the pruning*. There are two types of pruning: thinning and pinching.

THINNING. Thinning involves inspecting each branch on the vine. Vines are going to do what they're made to do—grow. They easily become quite wild, with vines rambling and tangling rapidly. The gardener must inspect all the plants to determine which branches will bear the best fruit, survive the elements, and handle environmental stress. A vine only has so many units of energy, and the gardener wants as much of it as possible to be directed toward producing good fruit. So they cut away the dead stock and remove the weaker vines, making room for the stronger to grow healthy.

When I meet with people who are seeking counseling and spiritual guidance, they often reel off a healthy list of priorities. But then I'll ask them, "Show me your schedule." Because it's what we put down in ink, on our calendars, that reveals what we are truly prioritizing.

One of my mentors once said that scheduling was one of the most spiritual acts a Christ follower can ever do. This is our chance to declare daily, weekly, monthly, and yearly what we honestly value. Many of us are constantly overcommitting, and it's costing us our health. And if we're honest, we feel like we're running on fumes. The gardener wants to trim the energy drainers out from your calendar, to help you reprioritize in order to bear the best kind of fruit in your life.

What is the best kind of fruit? That which thrives through every season, crisis, and circumstance.

If you were to give God the shears, are there any branches in your life that need to be thinned out? Any places where you have overcommitted yourself and are unable to give your very best? Think of what would happen if you could put those units of energy toward what you're really passionate about.

Imagine the possibilities.

When Theo Epstein left the Boston Red Sox to be the general manager of the Chicago Cubs, he preached this message over and over: trust the process. He believed deeply that if the team stayed committed to the plan, they would win a World Series. And in 2016, after 108 years without that trophy, they finally won it. To the surprise and amazement of every Cubs fan!

PINCHING. As I mentioned, the second way a gardener will prune is by doing what they call "pinching." Every branch of the vine has a shoot that grows up, and those shoots are what produce the grapes. Gardeners don't want grapes to grow randomly. Sometimes if the grapes grow too quickly and a storm comes through, they will not be strong enough to survive. Sometimes the shoots overproduce, sometimes not enough. Young rushed grapes will produce a bitter wine. So gardeners pinch the shoots, creating a source of growth so that more of the vines, sustenance and energy can build up, providing these grapes the very best nutrition to thrive.

Essentially what the gardener is saying to the branch is "Not now!"

A mentor once told me, "God usually answers our prayers with three responses—yes, no, and not now."

For some of us this year, we were all ready to go. That dream vacation. The new business idea. The long-anticipated wedding ceremony. A new job. But out of the blue a pandemic descended, and we were forced to hear the words "not now."

What gets even more difficult is when we look at someone else, whether on social media or on our team or in our family, who seems to be producing and thriving. It's hard for the human soul when God says "Not now" to us and "Yes" to someone else. But what if we actually trusted the gardener?

What if we truly believed that this wasn't some kind of punishment, as many sincere Christ followers are often all too quick to believe, but rather God preparing us for something more?

While staying at the cottage on the vineyard, I asked the vinedresser, who owned the vineyard, how long it took after a vine was planted before it would bear fruit.

"Three years," he said.

Quick question. How long was Jesus with his disciples?

Yep, three years! And coming to the end of his time on earth, Jesus stopped where? At a vineyard. Where he told his disciples, "Friends, after three years, it's time for you to bloom."

Let's follow this vine a little further.

It takes three years for a vine to bear fruit. During that time, the gardener is cutting, pruning, thinning, and pinching. Next he takes those grapes and puts them through the winemaking process. Grapes are washed and smashed, bottled up and shipped out to line the shelves of stores all over the world. A really good bottle of wine gets purchased and then put away in a cellar for a few more years. All in all, that's about a nine-year process to produce a good bottle of wine.

In early Hebrew society, a bottle of wine was a symbol of blessing, favor, and joy. But it also represented hope. Every bottle of wine was a picture of hope because it represents years of belief that something good would come from the pruning and thinning of those branches. To the person reading this who feels stuck in an acutely painful part of your story, I know this doesn't make sense right now, but I also know you will come to the other side of this.

It can take years of pruning and thinning to create an incredible bottle of wine and enjoy it on the other side of our pain.

The vineyard process is also the story of how God is forming, shaping, thinning, pruning, and molding you to become a fantastic bottle of wine. Once again let me remind you—we can*not* microwave spiritual formation. It takes time to grow, to heal, to mend, to discover your passions, your prejudices, your fears and hopes, your strengths and weaknesses, just like a good bottle of wine.

In verse 5 Jesus said, "I am the vine; you are the branches. If you remain in me and I in you, you will bear much fruit; apart from me you can do nothing."

Apart from Jesus you can do nothing. Do you really believe that?

If we're honest, there are probably times when we've lived in such a way that proclaimed, "I am the vine, and Jesus, you are a branch, and if you don't bear fruit in my life, I will cut you off."

Jesus is trying to reframe for us that he is the vine. He is the one who gives us our sustenance and energy. He is the one who allows us to bear fruit. Apart from Christ we can do nothing sustainable over time. Nothing that will last. Nothing that will flourish past our life, no legacy, no bottle on the shelf. And don't we want to leave the kind of legacy that our kids and grandkids, our community, and our church family will cherish and respect? When you keep your focus on living in alignment with Jesus, you will leave a profound legacy because you will bear the best kind of fruit.

But I know many of you might be listening saying, "But you don't know what I've done! You don't understand how I have sabotaged relationships with family members" or "You don't know how I have wrecked my marriage [or business, or friendships] due to brokenness and sin."

Please hear me say this: I hear you and I still love you. God knows everything—everything!—you've done, dreamed, wished, and thought. And yet, he proclaims his love over you for all of eternity. I may not know what you've done, but God does. And he loves you just the same.

WEEP AND BLEED. Have you ever wondered how wines can be blended from two types of grapes? The gardener cuts off the vine way down low at the base, where branches are being produced. Then the vine begins to "weep and bleed" (actual vinedresser language). The gardener proceeds to make a "T-cut" in the middle of the vine. After waiting several days, the gardener then adds the new seeds of the grapes they want to merge with the vine. Then they bandage the seeds in the T-cut and a few days later remove the bandage. Three years later, if done properly, the vine is bearing new fruit!

I don't know about you, but when I hear that, I hear the *gospel*.

This is my story!

My brokenness, my sin, my shame, all the wrongs I have committed toward God, myself, others, and this world were placed into that T-cut known as the cross. And the Holy Spirit began a new work in me. I went from fear to love, from despair to joy, from anxiety to peace, from stress to patience, from anger to kindness, from pride to goodness, from jealousy to faithfulness, from fits of rage to gentleness.

This is what God does. This is what the Divine Gardener is continuing to do for me.

And this is what he can and will do for you.

Will you let him?

This is his promise: If you remain in Jesus, you will bear much fruit. You will bear the fruit of the Spirit. Can you even imagine what this might mean in your one heaven-sent life? What might it do for every relationship you have? What might it feel like to be whole, holy, and spiritually healthy?

It begins with a choice. Choose to trust.

Trust the pruning.

Trust the process.

Trust the promise.

In January 2018, the UK appointed Tracey Crouch as the newly created minister of loneliness. Seriously. Imagine that title on your LinkedIn profile. The UK realized they had a loneliness problem. In 2017, a report detailed that "200,000 people had not had a conversation with a friend or relative in more than a month."[1]

The report further astonished, showcasing that $3.5 billion was lost each year due to loneliness, over nine million Brits often or always felt lonely, and 43 percent of seventeen- to twenty-five-year-olds struggled with loneliness.[2] Mark Robinson, the chief officer of Age UK, which is the largest charity working with older people in Britain, said about loneliness, "It's proven to be worse for health than smoking 15 cigarettes a day."[3]

This is true of the UK, but likely also holds true in America. Yes, even in the church.

In the early church, we see countless appeals by the leaders of the day for people to embrace their communities, to gather together, and to live life side by side in support and love. Look at Colossians 3:13: "Bear with each other and forgive one another if any of you has a grievance against someone. Forgive as the Lord forgave you." Or Galatians 6:2: "Carry each other's burdens, and in this way you will fulfill the law of Christ." In Acts 2:44–47 we read that the early church looked a lot like a community who embraced these values: "All the believers were together and had everything in common. They sold property and possessions to give to anyone who had need. Every day they continued to meet together in the temple courts. They broke bread in their homes and ate together with glad and sincere hearts, praising God and enjoying the favor of all the people. And the Lord added to their number daily those who were being saved."

This is a beautiful and compelling picture of what the church can be. Yet, if we're being honest, often we encounter a much different reality within its walls. Stories of dysfunction, misinformation, abuse, dishonesty, and corruption fan the headlines. Less newsworthy experiences of judgment and spiritual shunning are just as damaging to the people who make up the body of the church. According to a 2019 Gallup poll, "Not only are millennials less likely than older Americans to identify with a religion, but millennials who are religious are significantly less likely to belong to a church. Fifty-seven percent of religious millennials belong to a church, compared with 65% or more in older generations."[4] If the church was meant to be a place of fellowship and our world is lonelier than ever, we have to beg the question of why. Why is this the case? What has happened to cause this decline? Where is the church missing the mark to create community to soothe this loneliness pandemic? And most important, how do we remedy the problem so it can be all that Jesus intended for it to be?

Recently I was in Santa Cruz, California, an amazing little surf town nestled an hour or so from San Francisco. The city is quite unique because you can surf in the morning and then drive a mile and half from the beach to wander through a massive old-growth redwood forest. When you walk among these ancient giants, you get the feeling you're thousands of feet up in the mountains, but Santa Cruz is only four hundred feet above sea level. The cooling fog that comes in off the Pacific Ocean creates a perfect environment for redwood trees to thrive.

My buddy Danny took me surfing while I was there. We jumped in his dusty blue 1960s Ford pickup and went mountain biking through the redwood forest. After a few minutes of hearing my friend share bits about what makes the redwoods so special, my interest was piqued and I knew I would be pulling another all-nighter, researching.

And I came to discover that redwoods love to chase the light. They grow about ten feet a year and get 40 percent of their water from drinking the fog. Scientists will tell you that their trunks are filled with eight thousand gallons of water. Talk about a savings account!

Redwoods can survive any drought. Their bark is fire resistant, bug resistant, and excellent for construction purposes. Redwoods are the tallest trees and some of the oldest living trees on the planet. Because they are almost four hundred feet tall, you would think that their root system would go down some two hundred feet into the earth. But here's the crazy thing. Their roots only go down somewhere between nine and twelve feet. *Nine and twelve feet.*

It's been observed that when a redwood tree is planted by itself, it will not withstand even a slight wind. That young tree will topple right over. All its weight is just too much for those shallow roots to bear. But when planted together with other redwoods, they withstand every fierce element. Scientists have been able to discover that their roots go down nine to twelve feet, and then they *go out another one hundred feet* looking for other redwoods to interlock their roots with.

What allows these trees to withstand the elements is their interconnectedness.

I once had a friend who had been sober for over twenty-nine years yet still went to Alcoholics Anonymous meetings regularly. Once I'd asked him why he still made it a point to go, with all those years of sobriety under his belt. His response was one I'll never forget. "Every time I show up to a meeting," he said, "there will be some kid coming for the first time, or a mother finally naming her addiction, or a father at the end of his rope. And I want to make sure they see that the program can work. That there is hope. Because if we make it, then I make it."

If we make it, then I make it.

So beautiful! This is exactly what scientists are discovering to be the mantra of redwoods. They not only interconnect with one another but they share their resources. If one tree is sick or struggling, it sends out a signal through its root system, and the other trees will redirect their nutrients to sustain the weaker one. Scientists note that these giant redwoods share a special sort of language known only to them.

Here's what I need you to understand. Christianity is not a solo sport.

You won't make it if you try to do this all on your own. Those potholes will become sinkholes and create more suffering for you and those you care most about. It's when we stand together, walk together, and go through the process of sanctification together that our lives take on such richness.

Jesus taught us to love one another. The phrase "one another" is used almost a hundred times in the New Testament alone. When you read through the Bible, you see this phrase again and again.

Andy Stanley said, "The primary activity of the local church is one anothering one another."[5]

We're called to:

Love one another.

Confess to one another.

Value one another.

Pray for one another.

Encourage one another.

Forgive one another.

Outdo one another in showing honor.

Bear with one another, spur one another on, as well as many, many more one-anothers.

If we make it, then I make it.

I once picked up a copy of Rob Lowe's autobiography at an airport bookstore after reading this opening line:

I think it was Alfred Hitchcock who said 90 percent of successful moviemaking is in the casting. The same is true in life. Who you are exposed to, who you choose to surround yourself with, is a unique variable in all of our experiences and it is hugely important in making us who we are. Seek out interesting characters, tough adversaries and strong mentors and your life can be rich, textured, highly entertaining and successful, like a Best Picture winner. Surround yourself with dullards, people of vanilla safety and unextraordinary ease, and you may find your life going straight to DVD.[6]

Straight to DVD is not where you want to go, friend. Who are you walking with during this season of your life? Who have you opened up to and allowed to see the struggles and more imperfect parts of you?

Who are you confessing to?

Who is confessing to you?

Just before sunrise on my last day in Santa Cruz, I made my way back to the forest and stood in the middle of a circle of stately redwoods. Lying on the ground, I stared up at the tops of these giants, each branch covered in golden morning light.

I was startled by a state park worker on his morning patrol who stopped to say hello, and we got to talking. I asked him why this grove of trees was formed into an open circle. He explained that when one tree falls, its seeds begin to scatter. And because it is still connected to other roots, its neighboring trees send out nutrients to the new baby offspring. Which causes new life to grow from the fallen tree. "Pretty cool, huh?" he said, with enthusiasm.

Before I could help myself, I blurted out, "That's a picture of the gospel! On Good Friday it looked like death had won, but heaven was just getting started. Resurrection power came through, and Jesus came alive. That's what Easter is all about. We have that same resurrection power available for us."

I was sure I'd freaked him out, but he just looked at me and slowly said, "I've never thought of that, but I wonder if that's why scientists refer to this circular formation of redwoods as a *cathedral*. Such a truly unique and holy space."

Can you even?

When we listen to our pain.

When we get courageously curious about the why behind our fears.

When we let others see our weakest places.

When we let go of that old pain that's no longer serving us.

When we tell the truth.

When we drop the mask.

When we submit to the pruning and make room for the hope.

When we gather together and share with those in need.

We become the church.

The thing beneath the thing, the buried hurts and fears that motivated and informed much of your narrative in the past, once seen and named, evolve to become part of an extraordinary root system, one that forever binds us together as brothers and sisters in Christ.

What was once a gaping sinkhole births a forest of connection. The thing beneath the thing becomes the *roots beneath the soil* that hold us up, together creating a potential cathedral for all to experience.

DIG A LITTLE DEEPER

1. Where have you experienced God's pruning recently in your life?
2. When you are in a season of waiting or trusting the process, how does that make you feel?
3. Which of God's promises are you needing to remember?
4. Who are the redwoods in your life that are helping you get after the thing beneath the thing?
5. Look at the "one anothers" in the New Testament and ask God which three of these you do really well and which three you need to work on in this coming season.

BENEDICTION

A FEW SUMMERS AGO, MY SON, EMERSON, AND I SPENT every Tuesday serving in a local food pantry. Each morning we gathered with others to find out our assignments and to hear a story from one of the volunteers. One Tuesday, an especially energetic volunteer named Tom shared his excitement about a "release party." At first, I wondered if someone near and dear to him had been incarcerated, or maybe someone was graduating from a substance abuse program.

But no, he wanted to invite our team of volunteers to his house to celebrate the hundreds of monarch butterflies he had raised and was now releasing into the wild.

I had never heard of anything like this. I remembered going to a butterfly garden once at a zoo but never knew someone who raised them in their home. Tom was an amazing guy, the kind of person who really paid attention to others. He greeted each and every person in the food pantry with a smile and took the time to ask how they were doing. He was humble and curious and filled with sincerity.

I love learning from someone who knows about topics I know nothing about. Like the butterflies. Tom's enthusiasm convinced me butterflies were exciting. After we finished serving that day, Emerson and I went to Barnes & Noble to begin researching caterpillars and monarchs. I wanted to understand what fascinated Tom so much that he was throwing a release party.

The first book I bought was *The Very Hungry Caterpillar* by Eric Carle. Okay, not really! But that children's book is pretty spot-on when it comes to how caterpillars love to eat. Scientists tell us this creature can destroy a garden in one day because it eats and eats and eats non-stop. Without the ability to control this impulse, caterpillars basically eat themselves out of their skin. They do this five times. Eat and shed their skin. Eat and shed their skin. Eat and shed their skin. Eat and shed their skin. Eat and shed their skin. But for some reason, after the fifth cycle, they move to a safe tree or plant to undergo a transformation.

While studying this, I learned that when a caterpillar enters the chrysalis stage, it has only fifty cells. Fifty. You'd think a creature that eats itself through a hometown buffet would have more than that in its stomach alone!

But something amazing happens to this fifty-cell eating machine. A green goo overtakes it, and it goes from fifty cells to fifty thousand. The caterpillar does not just shift—it becomes something entirely new.

For approximately twelve days, the morphing caterpillar remains in the chrysalis, until one day it has the strength to break out. As it struggles and fights to do so, something else happens.

It realizes it has wings.

Can you imagine if you were Joe Caterpillar and, having crushed an entire garden in one afternoon, you took a two-week-long pause only to suddenly realize, *Oh . . . oh, wow, man. I've got wings*?

For the next couple of hours, this new creation begins to stretch its wings and dry them off. Depending on the time of year it emerges from its chrysalis, the monarch butterfly may immediately join thousands of others on a migration that will take it from the midwestern United States and Canada—all the way to Mexico.

Isn't that amazing? Hours ago, it had been in a sleeping bag, thinking it was a caterpillar. And now—boom!—it's off.

"Where are you going, bro?"

"I'm going to Mexico."

"Yeah, me too! I'm going to Mexico."

"Hey, let's all go to Mexico!"

"Viva México!"

And away they go.

Somehow, both in the process of breaking from the chrysalis and during the flight itself, these creatures develop the strength they need. For nearly sixty days, they fly an average of fifty to one hundred miles a day.

Here's another amazing thing. They do have to stop along the way to rest and eat. But you know where they stop, right? They land on flowers. And they pollinate as they go. They're on this epic journey with their new wings and sense of what they're made for, and along the way, they're sprinkling new life.

At the end of their transcontinental journey, hundreds of millions of monarch butterflies descend on the same tiny village of Cerro Prieto, Michoacán, high in a Mexican mountain range. The villagers have been expecting them. They've prepared a celebration. When the butterflies arrive, the music begins, and the people open their hearts to welcome these intrepid world travelers who have become so much more than what they were when they began.

When I discovered this, I could see why Tom was so passionate about his release party. As I kept thinking about the caterpillars—the metamorphosis, the chrysalis, the monarchs, the new creations, the journey, the pollination, and the party in Mexico—I saw the process of transformation.

This is what God wants to do in each of us: help us grow into our best selves and become whole, holy, and spiritually healthy.

Keep Fighting to Finish Well

We are midway through the year 2020 as I write this. As I think back, if someone had pulled me aside in late 2019 and told me that in the first few months of 2020, the Houston Astros appearance in the 2017 World Series would be questioned due to cheating, Prince Harry and Meghan Markle would exit the monarchy, and NBA legend Kobe Bryant would be killed along with his daughter and seven others in a tragic helicopter crash, I would have said, "You're pulling my leg." But if they had gone on to say that the world would be facing a pandemic, churches would not be able to gather in buildings for Easter, every sporting event would be suspended or canceled for the foreseeable future, and every state would participate in peaceful protests in response to the senseless murders of George Floyd, Breonna Taylor, Ahmaud Arbery, and thousands of others, I would have thought they had lost their mind.

Like most of us, I had great expectations for what the year 2020 should be, but I'm finding those to be way off from reality. Turning on the news, I hear every "un" word under the sun.

Unprecedented.

Unknown.

Unsure.

Unforgettable.

Uncontrollable.

Unexpected.

Unstable.

I'm not even sure what to type here as I attempt to list the number of people who've been infected with COVID-19. Suffice it to say, the number is staggering—multimillions—and growing every day. For some of us in the year 2020, we went from dropping off our kids at school and heading to the office to transforming our homes into offices and classrooms. Even now, with social distancing and masks and new vaccines, the pandemic is far from over. We all know what Zoom is now. Everything has changed.

I've often tried to imagine what the disciples were thinking and feeling as their time with Jesus was about to come to an end. But he knew. He knew the uncertainty. He knew the fear and anxiety barely hidden beneath the surface.

For many of us, when pressures grow or crises strike, one of the first priorities to go is our personal time with Christ. But Jesus told his disciples—over and over—to remain in him (John 15:4–10). The word *remain* is often translated "abide," which comes from the word *abode*, meaning "to make your home in." No matter what circumstances would soon be churning around his disciples, Jesus wanted them to keep the *remain* thing the main thing. He wanted us all to abide, abode, make our home in him.

Dallas Willard once said, "Spiritual formation is the process through which those who love and trust Jesus Christ effectively take on his character."[1] This is what I desire, for my heart to experience the power of restoration, to be rebuilt from the inside out, and to experience a kind of renewal that can only come from the Spirit. It's a long process with many rooms to go, but I'm praying that through this the way of Christ will reimagine and restore my heart.

I want this for you too. As you have marched through this book, you've wrestled with a fresh understanding of why we do what we do. You've discovered new strategies, actions, and tools for navigating and changing course when needed. Ultimately, we've talked about, around, and through the thing beneath the thing.

While playing basketball in college, I had to fly into Kansas with my team for an away game. We were underdogs. To Kansas State, Cal State Fullerton wasn't exactly intimidating. We were definitely not expected to win. As we came out for warm-ups, the Kansas student section shouted all kinds of trash talk our way. To be fair, what they were yelling was rather brilliant and pretty funny. A large group of students kept screaming "Coach's son!" at me because in their minds there was no way I should be on the team unless I was the coach's son. In the locker room between quarters, Coach Hawk had us close our eyes. For a minute I thought we were going to pray. Instead he started asking us questions.

"When you miss an open shot, how will you choose to respond?"

"When you turn the ball over, how will you choose to respond?"

"When the defense shifts from man to zone, how will you choose to respond?"

"When the student section mocks you continuously, how will you choose to respond?"

This was an ingenious exercise in visualizing and preparing for what might happen next, one I've never forgotten. To help anticipate my triggers, I've started reviewing my schedule ahead of time and pinpointing the spots where I'll be most susceptible to choosing hideouts, sinking into insecurities, or living under false narratives instead of grace. This practice has been amazingly helpful. I can often imagine how I might choose to keep the *remain* thing the main thing even when adversity strikes, stress rises, or my potholes get exposed.

Friends, God wants you to become whole, holy, and spiritually healthy. Recently I've been sitting with some of Paul's parting words to his mentee, Timothy. "I have fought the good fight, I have finished the race, I have kept the faith" (2 Tim. 4:7).

I so desperately want to be able to proclaim Paul's words toward the end of my life—to my God, to my wife, to my kids, to my friends, and to my family's legacy.

I fought the good fight.

I finished the race.

I kept the faith.

Leadership guru Bobby Clinton suggested that only a third of the biblical characters finished well.[2] The same thing Clinton found in his research holds true for pastors and Christian business leaders, politicians, and teachers. We all know leaders—people we once looked up to—who have chosen to hide and lie and manipulate instead of finishing the race well. They've chosen to reject grace and run away from the problems and pain they've created. I experienced this very publicly over the past few years during my work at Willow Creek Community Church. It has been excruciating to watch those I once respected crumble. Especially when I know there is more than enough grace to go around for those who choose to believe it.

But we are all at risk. I have realized I'm a prime candidate for experiencing it myself with events I'm just now beginning to put into words.

We need to be honest with God and ourselves. We have to want greater dependency and a deeper relationship with Christ. We have to want more for our futures than the world offers. If we don't desire to be different, we will go the way of those who falter. Life is a fight and a race. We have to choose to rise to the challenge, to exercise our faith daily. Only the faithful will finish strong in pursuit of the living God's will for their lives.

I meditate on Paul's words as my wife and I work on rehabbing our new old cabin. God's kindness and grace are continually revealing to me places where I need to lean hard into my faith. To keep fighting so I can finish well.

My brothers and sisters, may you be strong in grace and courageous in curiosity. May the Lord give you that Rak Chazak strength to not shy away from the potholes in your story. May he give you insight into how those potholes have become the setup that sets you off, moving in a direction farther away from Christ and his peace. May the Holy Spirit lead you to understand how your hideouts, insecurities, and narratives can turn potholes into dangerous sinkholes that will affect your ability to finish well.

May you have the desire and character to welcome everything that comes to you in this moment because you know it is for your healing.

May the relentlessness of grace never let you stay stuck. May you become deeply formed and renewed by the gift grace truly is. May you let it find you and have its way in you.

May you discover your need to keep the *remain* thing the main thing. And to be powerfully connected to and interlocked with the redwoods in your life.

The old you served you well through the injuries and challenges of your past, but that's not the you that's required for what will come next. Now is the time the world needs your true self, your whole heart, your greatest courage, and the fullness of your joy. We need your honesty, your healed story, and your dreams for what is to come.

Now that you know why you do what you do, you can use all you and I have learned to power forward with the fullness of God's grace. And the best part is, we get to do that together too.

From one redwood to another, well done.

ACKNOWLEDGMENTS

AS THE GREAT MICHIGAN FOOTBALL COACH BO Schembechler once said, "No man is more important than the team; no coach is more important than the team. The team, the team, the team!" I'm profoundly thankful for the team God has assembled to help make the thing beneath the thing happen.

First and foremost, thank you to Sarah, Emerson, and Mercy. I love you three more than anything else. You are God's greatest gift to me, and I hope these words make you proud.

Grateful to you, Alexander Field. You're more than my literary rabbi/agent; you have become a brother, my trusted friend, and someone I deeply respect. Grateful to have had your wisdom as well as the entire Bindery Agency team behind this project.

Thank you to my W publishing team for helping to make this such an enjoyable process! Damon Reiss, thanks for believing in this book. Debbie Wickwire, thanks for picking up all my calls and adding such perfect insights along the way. Dawn Hollomon, thanks for your edits and encouragement throughout the joy that is track changes. Caren Wolfe, Alex Woods, Kit Tosello, and Chasity Edwards, thank you immensely for all your hard work.

The past couple of years have not been the easiest; but God has surprised me with friends, mentors, partnerships, and communities that have truly helped me pick up the pieces.

A special thank you to:

The *Craft & Character* team: the leader of leaders Sean Morgan, aka Viper, Dick Anderson (also known as the best coach on the planet), and the rest of the CDF Capital fam.

The Home Team Podcast: Sam Acho, Trey Burton, and Sam Ponder. Grateful for the space to talk sports, faith, family, and culture. You each make me better and live this book out.

To the pastors who leaned in rather than out when my Willow life fell apart, I thank you. You took my calls, gave of your time, and were a fresh reminder of Jesus at a time when I needed it. Your church communities have been so very kind to me, and I will always think of them with gratitude in my heart. Thank you to Steve Poe and Northview Church, Carl Sutter and Foundations Church, Joel Thomas and Mission Community Church, Eric Parks, TJ Addington, and Heartland Community Church, and Ken Werlein and Faithbridge Church.

Thank you to Rick Warren, Erwin McManus, Max Lucado, Rob Bell, Annie F. Downs, Harvey Carey, Scot McKnight, Danielle Strickland, and Eugene Cho for your wisdom, phone calls, texts, and kindness along the way.

Thank you, Ann, for writing the foreword. I respect you and hold you in such high regard, not only because of your brilliant writing, but also because of who you are. When I saw you step aside at the Justice Conference and give the final teaching spot to a woman of color, I became one of your biggest fans. Thanks for sharing the light of Jesus with all of us!

Grateful for my family and the friendships that have deepened in this desert season. Adam and Jenny, Blaine and Margaret, Eric Parks, Joel Thomas, Boomer Roberts, Josh Turner, Tyler Reagin, Brad Lomenick, Mike and Jen Minarsich, Konnie Allee, Judy Carter, Tommy Nixon, Jay Hewitt, Kevin Mo-Wong, and so many more. Love you all more than you will ever know.

Love you, Dad. Wish I could hand you this book. Think you would have loved it.

Jim Harbaugh, Juwan Howard, and JJ McCarthy for bringing some future championships back to Ann Arbor. Go Blue!

NOTES

Foreword

1. JoAnna Klein, "Tree Stumps Are Dead, Right? This One Was Alive," *New York Times*, July 25, 2019, https://www.nytimes.com/2019/07/25 /science/tree-stump-alive.html; Ed Yong, "The Stump That Didn't Die," *The Atlantic*, July 25, 2019, https://www.theatlantic.com/science/archive /2019/07/mystery-undead-tree-stump/594673/.

2. David Nield, "Scientists Find Weird, Zombie-Like Tree Being Kept Alive by a Forest 'Superorganism,'" Science Alert, July 29, 2019, https:// www.sciencealert.com/this-tree-stump-is-mysteriously-being-kept -alive-with-a-little-help-from-its-friends.

Chapter 1: Why Do I Do Those Things I Do?

1. Richard Rohr, "Transforming Our Pain," Center for Action and Contemplation, September 18, 2020, https://cac.org/transforming-our -pain-2020–09–18/.

2. Mary Mrozowski, *The Welcoming Prayer*, sermon notes (Chapel Hill, NC: Chapel of the Cross, 2012), https://thechapelofthecross.org/wp-content /uploads/2012/11/140228-with-DFsermonWelcoming-Prayer.pdf.

Chapter 2: Potholes, Triggers, and Responses

1. Mary Wisniewski, "Chicago Fills 108,000 Potholes This Year in 'Normal' Season, but 1 Crater Shows Gap in How City Handles Them,"

Chicago Tribune, March 2, 2018, https://www.chicagotribune.com/news /ct-met-chicago-potholes-20180226-story.html.

2. "Pothole Tracker," Transportation, City of Chicago, https://www.chicago .gov/city/en/depts/cdot/dataset/potholetracker.html.

3. Chicago Department of Transportation, "Pothole Repairs Frequently Asked Questions," Chicago City Hall, March 21, 2020, https://311 .chicago.gov/s/article/Pothole-repairs-frequently-asked-questions ?language=en_US.

4. Ernest Harsch, "The World Reflects on Rwanda Genocide," United Nations Africa Renewal, April 2004, https://www.un.org/africarenewal /magazine/april-2004/world-reflects-rwanda-genocide.

Chapter 3: Where We Go to Hide

1. Timothy J. Keller, *Counterfeit Gods: The Empty Promises of Money, Sex, and Power, and the Only Hope That Matters* (New York: Penguin Books, 2011), xxiv.

2. Liz Knueven, "The Average Credit Card Interest Rate by Credit Score and Card," *Business Insider*, January 25, 2021, https://www.businessinsider .com/personal-finance/average-credit-card-interest-rate.

3. "Advertising Spending of Selected Credit Card Issuers in the United States in 2019," Statistica, July 2020, https://www.statista.com/statistics /308842/ad-spend-credit-card-issuers-usa/.

4. C. S. Lewis, *Mere Christianity* (New York: HarperOne, 2001), 44.

Chapter 4: When Identity Becomes Insecurity

1. To learn more about the Enneagram, see "How the Enneagram System Works," the Enneagram Institute website, https://www .enneagraminstitute.com/how-the-enneagram-system-works.

2. "Ephesus Theatre," Ephesus.us, accessed March 31, 2021, https://www .ephesus.us/ephesus/theatre.htm.

3. James Barr, "The Hebrew/Aramaic Background of 'Hypocrisy' in the Gospels," in *Bible and Interpretation: The Collected Essays of James Barr*, ed. John Barton, vol. 2, *Biblical Studies* (Oxford, UK: Oxford University Press, 2013), 285.

4. Steve Tignor, "Rewatch, French Open 1990: Agassi Almost Flips Wig in First Slam Final," Tennis.com, May 27, 2020, https://www.tennis.com

/pro-game/2020/05/rewatch-french-open-1990-agassi-almost-flips-wig
-first-slam-final/88939/.

Chapter 5: From Insecurity to Envy

1. Ancient History Encyclopedia, s.v. "Solomon," by John S. Knox, January 25, 2017, https://www.ancient.eu/solomon/.
2. Ancient History Encyclopedia.
3. Wikipedia, s.v. "Thou Shalt Not Covet," last modified November 18, 2020, 08:36, https://en.wikipedia.org/wiki/Thou_shalt_not_covet.
4. Ben Carlson, "Perception Matters," A Wealth of Common Sense, November 13, 2014, https://awealthofcommonsense.com/2014/11 /relative/.
5. Vanessa Diffenbaugh, *The Language of Flowers: A Novel*, repr. ed. (New York: Ballantine Books, 2012), 312.

Chapter 6: Biases That Drive Narratives

1. Sendhil Mullainathan, "Racial Bias, Even When We Have Good Intentions," *New York Times*, January 3, 2015, https://www.nytimes .com/2015/01/04/upshot/the-measuring-sticks-of-racial-bias-.html.
2. Alan Schwarz, "Study of N.B.A. Sees Racial Bias in Calling Fouls," *New York Times*, May 2, 2007, https://www.nytimes.com/2007/05/02/sports /basketball/02refs.html.
3. Lisa Rapaport, "Nonwhite Patients Get Less Pain Relief in U.S. Emergency Rooms," *Physicians Weekly*, July 2, 2019, https://www .physiciansweekly.com/nonwhite-patients-get-less/.
4. Rapaport, "Nonwhite Patients Get Less Pain Relief."
5. Rapaport, "Nonwhite Patients Get Less Pain Relief."

Chapter 7: Let Grace Find You

1. "Jesus Christ," MP3 audio, track 3 on Brand New, *The Devil and God Are Raging Inside Me*, Interscope, 2007.
2. Brennan Manning, *All Is Grace: A Ragamuffin Memoir* (Colorado Springs: David C. Cook, 2011), np.
3. "The Sermons of John Wesley—Sermon 43: The Scripture Way of Salvation," Wesley Center Online, http://wesley.nnu.edu/john-wesley /the-sermons-of-john-wesley-1872-edition/sermon-43-the-scripture -way-of-salvation/.

4. Eugene H. Peterson, *A Long Obedience in the Same Direction: Discipleship in an Instant Society* (Downers Grove, IL: InterVarsity Press: 2000), 17.
5. Dallas Willard, interview at Catalyst West 2010 conference (Orange County, CA: Mariners Church), video shared by Catalyst Leader, July 12, 2010, on YouTube, 2:12, https://www.youtube.com/watch?v=0n_nsEoQKhY&ab_channel=CatalystLeader.
6. Tom Frontier, "The Welcoming Prayer by Father Thomas Keating," My Shepherd King, January 13, 2018, https://www.myshepherdking.com/the-welcoming-prayer-by-father-thomas-keating/.

Chapter 8: Be Strong in Grace

1. Eliza Murphy, "Teacher Has Personalized Handshakes with Every One of His Students," ABC News, February 1, 2017, https://abcnews.go.com/Lifestyle/teacher-personalized-handshakes-students/story?id=45190825.
2. Biography.com Editors, "11 Famous 'Braveheart' Quotes," Biography.com, May 20, 2015, https://www.biography.com/news/braveheart-quotes-anniversary.
3. Dallas Willard, "Spiritual Formation: What It Is, and How It Is Done," Dallas Willard Ministries, https://dwillard.org/articles/spiritual-formation-what-it-is-and-how-it-is-done.
4. Willard, "Spiritual Formation."
5. Adapted from Frontier, "The Welcoming Prayer by Father Thomas Keating."

Chapter 9: It's Your Choice

1. Malcolm Gladwell, *Outliers: The Story of Success* (Boston: Little, Brown, 2008), 41.
2. Dr. Joel Hoomans, "35,000 Decisions: The Great Choices of Strategic Leaders," Leading Edge, March 20, 2015, https://go.roberts.edu/leadingedge/the-great-choices-of-strategic-leaders.

Chapter 10: The Power of Connection

1. Tara John, "How the World's First Loneliness Minister Will Tackle 'the Sad Reality of Modern Life,'" *TIME*, April 25, 2018, https://time.com/5248016/tracey-crouch-uk-loneliness-minister/.

2. John, "How the World's First Loneliness Minister."
3. Ceylan Yeginsu, "U.K. Appoints a Minister for Loneliness," *New York Times*, January 17, 2018, https://www.nytimes.com/2018/01/17/world /europe/uk-britain-loneliness.html.
4. Jeffrey M. Jones, "U.S. Church Membership Down Sharply in Past Two Decades," Gallup, April 18, 2019, https://news.gallup.com/poll/248837 /church-membership-down-sharply-past-two-decades.aspx.
5. Andy Stanley talk at the re:group Conference, 2013.
6. Rob Lowe, *Love Life* (New York: Simon & Schuster, 2014), 1.

Conclusion

1. Dallas Willard, *The Great Omission: Reclaiming Jesus's Essential Teachings on Discipleship* (New York: HarperCollins, 2006), 80.
2. J. Robert Clinton, *Finishing Well—Six Characteristics*, 2007, http:// storage.cloversites.com/missouristateassociationoffreewillbaptists /documents/Finishing-Well-Six-Characteristics.pdf.

ABOUT THE AUTHOR

STEVE CARTER IS A PASTOR, SPEAKER, AUTHOR, PODCAST host, and the former lead teaching pastor of Willow Creek Community Church in Chicago. He hosts the *Craft & Character* podcast, where he helps people get better at the art of communication while ensuring their character always leads the way. His desire is to bring Jesus into every conversation and space he occupies. Steve cohosts one of the top sports podcasts, called *The Home Team Podcast*, which unpacks the intersection between faith, culture, sports, and family. With a degree in biblical studies from Hope International University, Steve has a heart for the local church. Currently an itinerant preacher and teacher for influential churches, conferences, events, camps, and retreats all over the country, Steve lives in Phoenix with his wife, Sarah, and their two kids.